STUDIES ON
FINANCIAL MARKETS
IN EAST ASIA

STUDIES ON FINANCIAL MARKETS IN EAST ASIA

Masayuki Susai
Shigeru Uchida

Nagasaki University, Japan

editors

 **World Scientific**

NEW JERSEY · LONDON · SINGAPORE · BEIJING · SHANGHAI · HONG KONG · TAIPEI · CHENNAI

Published by

World Scientific Publishing Co. Pte. Ltd.

5 Toh Tuck Link, Singapore 596224

USA office: 27 Warren Street, Suite 401-402, Hackensack, NJ 07601

UK office: 57 Shelton Street, Covent Garden, London WC2H 9HE

British Library Cataloguing-in-Publication Data

A catalogue record for this book is available from the British Library.

ISBN-13 978-981-4343-36-7

ISBN-10 981-4343-36-6

Printed in Singapore by B & Jo Enterprise Pte Ltd

Preface

During these decades, emerging economies have gradually shown the impressive pavement of their development to all over the world. Asian areas could also prevail steadily the same trends especially in China, India and the like. The movements might not always limit their influence to the large countries and manufacturing industry sectors. The financial services industries have been promoted together with and owing to the success of the vigorous leading industries of developing economies.

Though peoples have really observed these economic transitions from developing stages to developed ones not merely in East Asia but in other regions of Southeast Asia, we have conducted the studies investigated these years mainly about the field of East Asia, and focused on such topical issues as the money, banking and financial markets.

This book contains interesting 10 papers by professors and researchers to investigate contemporary financial matters in East Asian financial affairs in the markets and to present their research results shown in the table of contents.

In these several years we have managed to hold annual international academic conferences on Asian Financial Markets to exchange our researches here in Nagasaki, 2005-2009, and Fukuoka, 2010, in order to cultivate this line of studies in modern financial and accounting fields. From 2008 the activity of the conference has been supported by GP (Good Practice of Education and Research of Graduate School) of Japanese Ministry of Education, Science, Culture, Sport and Technology, and we highly appreciate the support.

We would also like to welcome readers' comments on papers here, and express our thanks to all who gave us their efforts to make the publication of this book possible.

Editors

SUSAI, Masayuki
Trustee and Professor, Nagasaki University

UCHIDA, Shigeru
Professor, Nagasaki University

Contents

Chapter 1

Multi Foreign Exchange Rate Relations in Turbulent Market: Lessons from Lehman Shock[*]

Masayuki Susai

Nagasaki University,
Trustee and Vice President

Abstract

As US Dollar, Euro and Japanese Yen are most heavily traded financial asset in the world, it must be difficult to find arbitrage opportunity. But in the case of Lehman Brothers problem, arbitrage opportunity might be occurred. The purpose of this paper is to see what's going on in turbulent market such as Lehman Brothers' shock in most heavily traded foreign exchange market.

We use ultra high frequency foreign exchange rate, its trading volume and orderflow indicator to compare the relations among three currencies in ordinary and turbulent period. We use the results in ordinary period as benchmark. With VAR, Vector Error Correction and GARCH model, we found that volume and volatility of three foreign exchange rates are highest in turbulent period. The relations among three currencies are different especially for EUR/JPY from VEC model. USD based rate did not affect on EUR/JPY in turbulent period, whereas USD based rate had clear effect on EUR/JPY during benchmark period. With the VAR and Granger Causality, we found that relations in volume and orderflow are weaker in turbulent period. Volatility covariance is highest in turbulent period but the causality is weak in this period (t-GARCH model).

---

[*] The financial support from Grant-in-Aid for Scientific Research (B), 15203016 (Japan Society for the Promotion of Science) is acknowledged. Comments and Discussions at 21st Asian Conference on International Accounting Issues are gratefully acknowledged.

Triangular arbitrage relations suggest that foreign exchange rates among three currencies are highly connected. In benchmark period, we can confirm that there exist long run relations among these three foreign exchange rates. But in turbulent period, these relations were weak or disappeared. These weak relations among three currencies can be understood that there exist arbitrage opportunities in turbulent period.

1. Introduction

US Dollar, Euro and Japanese Yen are most heavily traded financial asset in the world. So, it must be difficult to find arbitrage opportunity or misprice. Even if there exists this opportunity, it can alive quite a short. Under this consideration, s big country (market) specific event in US Dollar market may have dominant effect on world FX market. In other words, foreign exchange rate against USD may work as price leadership. Lehman Brothers problem in 2008 can be the candidate for this kind of event.

In this case, foreign exchange rates against US Dollar move first, then other rates will be tuned according to triangular arbitrage rate. If a lot dealer expects the US Dollar depreciation, almost all currency will appreciate against USD.   Cross rates among non USD currencies moves in either way depending on the relative magnitude of appreciation against USD. If the relations among US Dollar based exchange rates are stable, then it is easier to predict the direction of the movement of foreign exchange rates among non US Dollar currencies. If these relations are weak, then it's hard to see what's going to be happened. In latter case, arbitrage opportunities might be occurred even in heavily traded financial markets.

Such an event as economic indicator announcement has simple effect. This effect can be expected through economics. Lehman Brothers shock may have more complex effects. As for the Lehman Brothers shock, no one can expect what's going on not only in the US but also in the world. We were expecting that stock market would suffer big damage. But we did not know what kind of effect can be generated on FX market. Though there are so many papers on testing the relations between stock market and FX market, we do not reach a common understanding for this relation.

Here we are taking a closer look at this special event to find out the relations among these three currencies in terms of foreign exchange rate co-movement, trading activity transmission and volatility structure. So many papers have been published on the relations among multilateral currencies, information and foreign exchange rate. But it is hard to find the research which combines these two view points with ultra high frequent data as we describe below. Key note paper on volatility spillover in foreign exchange markets, Engle *et.al* (1990) were testing volatility spillover between different markets and between same markets in different days. They found that some news or events in a market transmitted to next market. So if a big event happens in Tokyo market, then this information has significant effect in London market and New York market sequentially. They did not test the relations among different markets in a same time zone and different currencies in a same market. Cai *et.al* (2001) picked very special event (only one day) in 1988 and tested the relations between foreign exchange volatility and market activity. We also pick very special event in this paper. But the event we pick here is the event we cannot expect how big it creates a dame on foreign exchange market and we use multilateral currencies relations to find out the effect of this event.

Recent researches on the volatility and information in foreign exchange market are testing whether information inflow have significant effect on foreign exchange movement and its volatility. The researches on foreign exchange market so far are using the number of news headlines on the Reuter screens, the number of quotes in given time interval (sometimes referred as trading activity or trade intensity) and representative trade volume. For example, even in resent papers , Evans and Lyons (2006) used order flow data from Citibank, and Frommel, Alexander and Menkhoff, (2007) obtains a transaction data from a bank. We call this kind of data as representative data in this paper. Brzeszczynski and Melvin, (2006) and Bauwends and Omrane and Giot, (2005),   Bauwens and Rime and Sucarrat, (2006), Frommel and Alexander and Menkhoff, (2007) utilize the number of trade in a given interval. Almost all papers commonly use the indicator of the volume, and count the number of quote in a given interval or they estimate the volume with some econometric models.

The rest of this paper contains four sections. In the next section, we present our special data in detail. In the section of our estimation and result, we show the clear impact of trading volume. We conclude our discussion in the last section.

2. Data

Real traded data is difficult to use in FX market. But in this paper, we use real traded data from ICAP named Data Mine ver.5 from EBS system. This data set provides us the foreign exchange rate traded, bid or ask indicator, volume and order book in 250 millisecond interval. As we know, so many dealers in banks and financial institutions in the world are trading through this EBS system run by ICAP. The earlier versions of Data Mine do not contain volume of each trade and order book.

In this paper, we construct 5 minutes interval data from 250 millisecond interval data. Data Mine ver.5 is nearly tick by tick data. But there might be more than 5 minutes between the trades especially in the interval of New York and Tokyo market time. In latter case, this series are not even spaced data and we may have difficulties to estimate econometric models. For these reasons, we construct even spaced data sets. Another reason for making even spaced data from tick-by-tick data is to compare different foreign exchange rate with multivariate time series model. If we use raw data, we are not sure that all trade in different foreign exchange rate occurs at same timing[1].

Our data spans from 1st of July to 30th of September in 2007 and 2008. The event we use here occurred in September, 2008. From July to September in 2008, we were suffering Subprime problem, we chose same period data in 2007 as the baseline for comparison. For using these months' data, we can control month of the year effect if exist.

In our research, we use Japanese Yen against US Dollar (US_JP), Euro against US Dollar (E_US) and Japanese Yen against Euro (E_JP).

---

[1] In these data sets, there exist weekends, national holidays or seasonality of the time of the day. We estimate a simple AR model with no trade dummy which covers all the no trade period regardless of the reason, no dummy variables are estimated significantly. With this result, we do not use any special treatment for no trade period im our data set. See Susai (2008).

US_JP and E_JP are nominated by JPY, and E_US are in USD term. We also use transaction volume and bid or ask indicator. Because the data we use is transaction data, we cannot use bid-ask spread. But with the bid or ask indicator, we affirm the direction of the transaction, buy trade or sell trade. For example, if the bid indicator is assigned to a US_JP, this means bid side of the foreign exchange rate is hit by the counter part of the transaction. This transaction may have downward pressure to the US_JP rate. For these reasons, we use these bid or ask indicators as the price pressure indicator and can be recognized as orderflow direction index.

Trading volume also has impact on price movement. Bigger volume usually has bigger impact on price movement. We sum up the total volume of bid transaction multiplied by bid indicator (-1) and ask transaction multiplied by ask indicator (1). This amount can be recognized as cumulative net orderflow in each 5 minutes. If this amount is positive, total buying orderflow in this interval is more than selling orderflow. This means upward pressure might be stronger in this interval.

Table 1. Financial Institution Failure in the US from July to September, 2008

Month	Date	Financial Institute
July	25	First National Bank of Nevada, First Heritage
Aug	1	First Priority
Aug	22	Columbia Bank and Trust
Aug	29	Integrity Bank
Sept	5	Silver State Bank
Sept	15	Lehman Brothers

Last year, six financial Institutions went to bankrupt or had fatal problem from July to September in the US. We pick one case in each month to see how the Lehman Brothers shock was special. In this paper, we use 15th and 16th as Lehman shock day data.

In Table 2, L_x means log difference of x, OF_x means orderflow of x and VOL_x means trading volume of x. The reason we choose 15th and 16th as Lehman shock day is that the mean number of trading volume in 15th is smaller than the number in 15th and 16th. The Lehman's news was released in New York day time. This means that dealers in Tokyo market and morning session of London could not catch this news. The reaction

M. Susai

to this news occurred just after the New York session in 15th. Morning session in Tokyo in 16th of September was the first dealing of the Tokyo market participants.

Table 2. Base Stat: Mean of Selected variables

	E_JP	E_US	US_JP	L_EJP	L_EUS	L_USJP	OF_E_JP	OF_E_US	OF_US_JP	VOL_E_JP	VOL_E_US	VOL_US_JP
2007	161.90	1.37	117.84	-9.3.E-07	2.8.E-06	-3.7.E-06	-0.65	0.34	-1.81	31.76	51.51	57.54
2008	161.78	1.50	107.54	-5.7.E-06	-5.8.E-06	-4.9.E-09	-0.58	0.62	0.79	25.41	97.89	66.02
Lehman	149.49	1.42	105.05	-2.3.E-05	-1.9.E-05	-3.8.E-06	-2.21	10.03	-5.47	47.40	152.59	127.62
22-Aug	162.31	1.48	109.41	3.1.E-05	-2.9.E-05	6.1.E-05	0.94	-4.48	7.27	20.79	78.18	53.59
25-Jul	168.59	1.57	107.38	2.3.E-05	4.9.E-06	1.8.E-05	-0.95	1.72	-1.23	24.70	80.58	67.53

From Table 2, it is obvious that trading volume and orderflow in Lehman case are biggest. Trading volume was about 100% more than that of the average in 2008 and 2007.

Table 3. Base Stat: Standard Deviation of Selected variables

	E_JP	E_US	US_JP	L_EJP	L_EUS	L_USJP	OF_E_JP	OF_E_US	OF_US_JP	VOL_E_JP	VOL_E_US	VOL_US_JP
2007	4.40	0.02	3.07	5.0.E-04	2.4.E-04	4.5.E-04	21.50	61.79	55.81	39.57	51.54	54.68
2008	6.82	0.06	1.60	6.0.E-04	4.7.E-04	5.5.E-04	18.28	60.70	48.14	32.13	102.46	64.56
Lehman	1.42	0.01	0.77	1.4.E-03	8.5.E-04	1.2.E-03	29.04	55.75	64.01	49.76	118.81	97.24
22-Aug	0.41	0.004	0.53	3.5.E-04	3.5.E-04	3.7.E-04	14.01	48.91	46.55	22.51	74.31	47.00
25-Jul	0.68	0.002	0.44	3.4.E-04	3.3.E-04	4.3.E-04	14.77	53.15	48.33	24.17	77.64	53.81

As for the standard deviation of each variable, the numbers of trading volume and log difference in Lehman shock are biggest. Because standard deviation of log difference of foreign exchange rate used to be referred as volatility, we can say that volatility was high and the transaction was heavy in FX market in Lehman shock days[2].

Table 4. Correlations between foreign exchange rates

	E_JP/E_US	E_JP/US_JP	E_US/US_JP	L_EJP/L_EUS	L_EJP/L_USJP	L_EUS/L_USJP
2008	0.94	0.25	-0.10	0.46	0.63	-0.29
	0%	0%	0%	0%	0%	0%
2007	0.32	0.89	-0.15	0.40	0.82	-0.06
	0%	0%	0%	0%	0%	0%
Lehman	0.64	0.81	0.06	0.49	0.74	-0.12
	0%	0%	12%	0%	0%	0%
25-Jul	0.11	0.95	-0.20	0.07	0.69	-0.58
	7%	0%	0%	27%	0%	0%
22-Aug	-0.75	0.93	-0.94	0.35	0.44	-0.56
	0%	0%	0%	0%	0%	0%

---

[2] The fact that high volatility comes with heavy trade is consistent with mixture of distribution hypothesis.

Table 4 shows the correlations among three currencies. Only the pattern in Lehman shock is different from the patterns in other periods.

Table 5. Correlations between foreign exchange rate and Orderflow/Volume

		E_JP	E_US	US_JP	L_EJP	L_EUS	L_USJP
2007	Orderflow	0.01	0.02	0.02	0.01	-0.03	-0.01
		24%	0%	1%	27%	0%	6%
	Volume	-0.25	-0.03	-0.18	-0.01	0.02	-0.01
		0%	0%	0%	22%	0%	7%
2008	Orderflow	0.04	-0.04	0.02	-0.04	0.01	-0.02
		0%	0%	1%	33%	33%	3%
	Volume	-0.27	-0.17	-0.22	-0.001	-0.02	0.01
		0%	0%	0%	92%	2%	12%
Lehman	Orderflow	0.12	0.06	0.01	-0.09	-0.02	-0.09
		0%	13%	90%	13%	61%	4%
	Volume	-0.31	-0.15	-0.23	0.02	-0.01	0.06
		0%	0%	0%	58%	85%	18%
25-Jul	Orderflow	-0.08	0.04	0.18	0.08	-0.17	-0.06
		18%	49%	0%	18%	0%	30%
	Volume	-0.04	0.23	-0.19	0.11	-0.06	0.06
		57%	0%	0%	7%	35%	36%
22-Aug	Orderflow	0.004	0.02	-0.06	-0.08	-0.07	-0.07
		95%	74%	35%	21%	29%	27%
	Volume	0.19	-0.12	0.004	-0.05	-0.05	-0.02
		0%	6%	95%	47%	43%	81%

As we mentioned earlier, orderflow and trading volume used to have some effect on the foreign exchange rate or its movement. In Lehman shock days, only the orderflow of E_JP has positive effect. Volume does not have any effect on foreign exchange rate movement in Lehman shock days. Also only the US_JP orderflow has significant effect on FX movement in Lehman shock days.

3. Model

The main objectives of this paper are to investigate the features of the relations among three major currencies in turbulent market in terms of foreign exchange rate movement, orderflow, volume and volatility. Orderflow and volume can be regarded as information inflow into market[3]. So, the structural features in these two variables may show the

---

[3] See Clark (1973).

information structure among these currencies. We should be careful that the information content of orderflow and volume might not clear in Lehman shock days.

Usual method to test relations between foreign exchange rates and those rates of change is Granger Causality test. If we want to focus on dynamic relations, we can use Vector Auto Regressive model. Before estimating these two models, we need to check the stationality of the data. As we expected, level of foreign exchange rates are I(1) and rate of change of FX is stational. Therefore, we need to employ Vector Error Correction model for foreign exchange rates[4]. In VEC model, we incorporate orderflow as exogenous variable[5].

$$\Delta FX_{it} = A_i EC_{it-1} + \sum B_{it} \Delta FX_{it-i} + C + \sum \Gamma_{it} OF_{it} + E_i \ , \quad E_i \sim iid \qquad (1)$$

Here FX_{it} consists of three foreign exchange rates, EC_{it} is error correction term, OF_{it} is orderflow vector and C is constant term.

$$X_{it} = \sum A_{it} X_{it-1} + E_i \ , \quad E_i \sim iid \qquad (2)$$

Here, X represents Volumes and Orderflows in three FXs. Because of the data stationality, we can apply Vector Autoregressive model for volume and orderflow data to figure out the dynamic structures among those.

The last model we will use for clarifying volatility structure, we employ tri-variate GARCH model to capture dynamic structure.

$$d \log(FX)_{it} = N_{it} + \sqrt{H_{it}} \ \Psi_{it}, \quad \Psi_{it} \sim N(0,1) \qquad (3)$$

$$H_{it} = \Omega\Omega' + A(d \log(FX)_{it-1} - N_{it-1})$$
$$(d \log(FX)_{it-1} - N_{it-1})' A' + BH_{it-1}B' \qquad (4)$$

Here, all variables are matrices. Ω is lower triangular vector, A and B are 3×3 diagonal vectors. With estimated $\tilde{h}_{it}$, which is a element of H_{it} in

---

[4] Before estimating VEC model, we have already conducted cointegration test and affirmed that there exist at least one cointegration vector.
[5] See the theoretical discussion, Killeen *et al.* (2006).

equation (4), we use the covariance of $\tilde{h}_{it}$ to find out the relations between volatilities and conduct Granger Causality test with the variance of $\tilde{h}_{it}$.

4. Results and Discussions

Table 6. Vector Error Correction Model

	2008			2007			Lehman		
	D(E_JP)	D(E_US)	D(US_JP)	D(E_JP)	D(E_US)	D(US_JP)	D(E_JP)	D(E_US)	D(US_JP)
A	-0.015*	3.93E-06	0.021*	-0.08*	0.000034	0.019*	-0.72*	-0.0003	0.31**
	0.01	0.0001	0.005	0.01	5.E-05	0.01	0.24	0.002	0.15
D(E_JP(-1))	-0.46*	0.0005*	0.006	-0.36*	0.0003*	0.028**	-0.221	0.0003	-0.27**
	0.02	0.0001	0.01	0.02	8.E-05	0.01	0.20	0.001	0.12
D(E_JP(-2))	-0.22*	0.0006*	-0.02*	-0.21*	0.0001**	-0.01**	-0.008	0.001**	-0.205*
	0.02	0.0001	0.01	0.02	7.E-05	0.01	0.14	0.001	0.08
D(E_US(-1))	43.35*	-0.12*	-2.14**	31.48*	-0.15*	-2.55	5.211	-0.108	20.612
	1.92	0.01	1.19	2.31	0.01	1.58	21.27	0.13	13.02
D(E_US(-2))	22.59*	-0.09*	1.79	21.45*	-0.05*	2.45	6.551	-0.16**	22.64*
	1.88	0.01	1.17	2.22	0.01	1.51	15.51	0.10	9.49
D(US_JP(-1))	0.52*	-0.0009*	-0.13*	0.37*	-0.0003*	-0.14*	0.031	-0.0004	0.173
	0.03	0.0002	0.02	0.02	0.00	0.02	0.28	0.002	0.17
D(US_JP(-2))	0.28*	-0.0007*	-0.03*	0.24*	-0.0001**	-0.02	0.130	-0.002	0.29*
	0.025	0.0002	0.016	0.023	1.E-04	0.016	0.202	0.001	0.124
C	-0.0005	-6.76E-06	6.62E-05	0.001*	4E-5**	0.0007*	0.0009	-0.0001*	0.009**
	0.001	4.E-06	0.0003	0.0004	2.E-06	3.E-04	0.007	0.0000	0.004
OF_E_JP	0.001*	7E-5*	0.0007*	0.001*	2E-5*	0.0006*	0.002*	9E-6*	0.001*
	3.E-05	2.E-07	2.E-05	2.E-05	9.E-08	2.E-05	0.0002	2.E-06	0.0001
OF_E_US	0.0003*	5E-5*	-0.0001*	0.0002*	3E-6*	-5E-6**	0.0005*	1.03E-5*	-0.0003*
	1.E-05	7.E-08	-6.E-06	7.E-06	3.E-08	5.E-06	0.0001	8.E-07	0.0001
OF_US_JP	0.0005*	-2E-6*	0.0005*	0.0005*	-4E-7**	0.0004*	0.0008*	-2.34E-5*	0.0007*
	1.20E-05	8.50E-08	7.50E-06	8.30E-06	3.60E-08	5.60E-06	1.10E-04	6.80E-07	6.50E-05
R-squared	0.33	0.39	0.36	0.48	0.43	0.45	0.37	0.29	0.34
F-statistic	963.85	1235.75	1081.97	1721.30	1422.89	1532.21	32.96	23.42	29.64
Log likelihood	22121.39	117086.60	31308.06	27440.03	130672.90	34716.75	237.44	3149.60	519.79

Significant level: *1% **5%
The figures unter the parameters are standard errors

Table 6 shows the results from VEC model. As we know, the value of A (coefficient of error correction terms) is indicating the convergence speed to long run equilibrium. In all periods, we can point out that there exist long run equilibrium relations between E_JP and US_JP, but not between E_JP and E_US, US_JP and E_US[6]. From these results, E_US

---

[6] As we apply ECM for E_JP and E_US, US_JP and E_US to figure out the long run equilibrium relations, we cannot find this relation between them.

rate does not have long run equilibrium relations to other two major foreign exchange rate.

The features of the parameters in Lehman shock days is that the magnitude of each parameters in Lehman shock days are about 10 times as big as those in 2008 and 2007. Results in 2008 and 2007 are quite similar. These results are indicating that the convergence speed of E_JP and US_JP is quite high in Lehman shock days.

Most important thing we need to address from these result is the causality relations from USD related rate to E_JP, non USD related rate. In the benchmark case (2007, 2008), USD related rates have clear effect on E_JP, and E_JP has some effect on USD related rates. But in Lehman period, we cannot find any effect from USD related rates to E_JP. Even lagged terms of E_JP do not have any effect on E_JP.

Table 7. Vector Auto Regression Model : Orderflow

	2008			2007			Lehma		
	OF_E_J	OF_E_U	OF_US_J	OF_E_J	OF_E_U	OF_US_J	OF_E_J	OF_E_U	OF_US_J
OF_E_JP(-1)	0.16	-0.04*	-0.0	0.08	0.09	0.07	0.32	-0.21	-0.1
	0.01	-0.025	-0.0	0.01	0.02	0.02	0.042	-0.08	-0.09
OF_E_JP(-2)	0.062	-0.0	0.01	0.03	-0.00	-0.0	0.03	-0.0	0.03
	0.01	-0.0	0.02	0.01	-0.0	-0.0	0.04	-0.0	0.10
OF_E_US(-1)	0.014	0.093	-0.00	0.008	0.11	0.01	0.01	0.14*	0.02
	0.00	0.01	-0.0	0.00	0.007	-0.00	0.02	0.042	0.05
OF_E_US(-2)	0.00	0.026	-0.01	-0.006*	0.03	-0.00	-0.044*	-0.0	-0.0
	2.2E-0	7.5E-0	-5.9E-0	-2.6E-0	7.4E-0	-6.7E-0	-2.1E-0	-4.2E-0	-4.8E-0
OF_US_JP(-1)	0.01	0.001	0.13	0.006*	0.01	0.109	-0.0	0.064*	0.102**
	2.85E-0	-9.64E-0	-7.59E-0	0.00	-0.0	-0.0	-0.0	0.04	0.04
OF_US_JP(-2)	-0.00	0.016*	0.06*	-0.007*	0.014	0.03	-0.032*	0.01	0.09**
	-0.00	0.010	0.008	0.003	0.009	0.008	-0.0	0.036	0.042
C	-0.46	0.48	0.64*	-0.57	0.38	-1.51	-1.2	9.02*	-4.1
	-0.1	0.44	0.34	-0.1	0.45	-0.4	-1.1	2.38	-2.7
R-squared	0.04	0.01	0.02	0.01	0.02	0.02	0.13	0.05	0.03
F-statistic	143.3	31.24	77.45	36.5	60.02	55.5	13.8	4.57	2.79
Log likelihood	-82403.1	-105712.9	-101138.6	-84996.2	-104955.8	-103039.2	-2713.2	-3113.8	-3198.4

Significant level: * 1%   * * 5%
The figures unter the parameters are standard errors

Table 7 shows the orderflow VAR model results. Interdependence pattern among three orderflows seems to be different between 2008, 2007 and Lehman shock days. In turbulent period, volume of E_US and US_JP do not have any effect on E_JP, non US Dollar based rate. To see the relations among three variables in detail, we conduct Granger Causality test with VAR model.

Table 8. Granger Causality test in Vector Auto Regression Model : Orderflow

| | | 2008 | | Lehman | |
Dependent	Independent	Chi-sq	Independent	Chi-sq
OF_E_JP	OF_E_US	43.28*	OF_E_US	4.59
	OF_US_JP	16.91*	OF_US_JP	3.63
	All	49.69*	All	8.90
OF_E_US	OF_E_JP	5.97*	OF_E_JP	8.27*
	OF_US_JP	3.14	OF_US_JP	3.56
	All	7.97	All	11.43**
OF_US_JP	OF_E_JP	0.32	OF_E_JP	2.44
	OF_E_US	3.05	OF_E_US	1.84
	All	3.37	All	4.24

Significant level: * 1%   ** 5%

As for the orderflow, interdependence structure among three foreign exchange rate is not clear and looks different in 2008 and Lehman shock days. In 2008, US Dollar based foreign exchange rate orderflows have impact on EUR/JPY transaction. But in turbulent market, we cannot find any clear structure among three major foreign exchange trades.

Table 9. Vector Auto Regression Model : Volume

| | 2008 | | | 2007 | | | Lehman | | |
	VOL_E_JP	VOL_E_US	VOL_US_JP	OF_E_JP	OF_E_US	OF_US_JP	OF_E_JP	OF_E_US	OF_US_JP
VOL_E_JP(-1)	0.47*	0.06**	0.05*	0.55*	0.045*	0.15*	0.42*	-0.05	0.06
	0.01	0.0288	0.02	0.01	0.02	0.02	0.063	-0.134	0.125
VOL_E_JP(-2)	0.203*	0.12*	0.00	0.206*	0.06*	-0.02	0.12**	0.22**	-0.11
	0.01	0.03	0.02	0.01	0.02	-0.02	0.06	0.13	-0.12
VOL_E_US(-1)	0.03*	0.59*	0.05*	0.065*	0.606*	0.08*	0.01	0.47*	-0.04
	0.003	0.009	0.007	0.007	0.009	0.010	0.02	0.05	-0.05
VOL_E_US(-2)	0.011*	0.209*	0.025*	0.015**	0.18*	0.01**	0.1*	0.34*	0.17*
	3.28E-03	9.15E-03	6.52E-03	0.01	0.01	0.01	0.02	0.05	0.05
VOL_US_JP(-1)	0.03*	0.08*	0.53*	0.031*	0.049*	0.51*	0.12*	0.28*	0.72*
	0.0	0.0	0.0	0.0	0.0	0.0	0.0	0.1	0.1
VOL_US_JP(-2)	-0.02*	-0.05*	0.14*	-0.02**	-0.03*	0.16*	-0.09*	-0.28*	-0.02
	0.01	0.02	0.01	-0.01	-0.01	0.01	-0.03	-0.07	-0.06
C	2.93*	12.37*	11.16*	2.84*	6.65*	8.86*	1.13	19.15*	20.21*
	0.22	0.61	0.43	0.26	0.33	0.36	2.35	4.96	4.64
R-squared	0.61	0.70	0.62	21.92	27.66	31.06	29.48	62.31	58.25
F-statistic	5085.03	7598.87	5245.00	7146.36	7816.84	6637.44	178.02	253.12	171.94
Log likelihood	-84500.11	-104167.70	-97678.89	7146.36	7816.84	6637.44	178.02	253.12	171.94

Significant level: * 1%   * * 5%
The figures unter the parameters are standard errors

Table 9 shows the VAR result with on relations among trading volume. With this result, interdependency of trading volume seems to be same. Difference might be the effect of Euro/JPY volume on USD/JPY volume.

Table 10. Granger Causality test in Vector Auto Regression Model : Volume

Independent	2008 Dependent	Chi-sq	Lehman Dependent	Chi-sq
VOL_E_JP	VOL_E_US	329.32*	VOL_E_US	30.75*
	VOL_US_JP	31.62*	VOL_US_JP	16.4*
	All	476.64*	All	45.51*
VOL_E_US	VOL_E_JP	51.24*	VOL_E_JP	3.01
	VOL_US_JP	28.56*	VOL_US_JP	22.67*
	All	131.27*	All	29.4*
VOL_US_JP	VOL_E_JP	11.97*	VOL_E_JP	0.73
	VOL_E_US	249.59*	VOL_E_US	15.94*
	All	349.11*	All	18.45*

Significant Level: * 1%   **:5%

The result of Granger Causality test is clear. In 2008, there exist endogenous relations among three foreign exchange rate trading volumes. This means high trading volume will be transmitted to other foreign exchange trading. But in turbulent market, only EUR/JPY volume does not affect other trading volume.

In the final part, we scrutinize the volatility relations among these three FXs. We adopt conditional variance from GARCH model as the volatility of FX rate of change.

Table 11. Tri-variate GARCH

	2008	2007	Lehman
MU(1)	-7.35E-05*	1.52E-06	-3.3E-05*
	3.39E-06	2.30E-06	4.78E-05
MU(2)	-1.11E-05*	4.29E-07	-2.29E-05*
	2.05E-06	1.30E-06	3.59E-05
MU(3)	-6.37E-05*	9.74E-07	-7.96E-06*
	3.92E-06	2.28E-06	4.15E-05
OMEGA(1)	3.33E-05*	5.28E-05*	2.08E-04*
	1.04E-06	7.07E-07	2.49E-05
OMEGA(2)	7.74E-06*	1.05E-05*	9.92E-05*
	1.29E-06	4.46E-07	2.02E-05
OMEGA(3)	3.39E-05*	4.16E-05*	1.67E-04*
	1.52E-06	7.13E-07	2.22E-05
OMEGA(4)	3.03E-05*	3.44E-05*	1.34E-04*
	9.89E-07	4.66E-07	1.89E-05
OMEGA(5)	-1.9E-05*	-3.12E-05*	-1.55E-05*
	1.40E-06	3.48E-07	1.50E-05
OMEGA(6)	-5.79E-07	2.14E-05*	-6.27E-06*
	4.35E-05	3.73E-07	2.E-02
ALPHA(1)	0.203*	0.26*	0.26*
	0.002	2.E-03	2.E-02
ALPHA(2)	0.34*	0.28*	0.25*
	0.003	2.E-03	8.E-03
ALPHA(3)	0.27*	0.28*	0.27*
	0.003	2.E-03	2.E-02
BETA(1)	0.98*	0.95*	0.95*
	3.E-04	5.E-04	6.E-03
BETA(2)	0.95*	0.95*	0.95*
	0.001	8.E-04	8.E-03
BETA(3)	0.97*	0.95*	0.94*
	3.E-04	2.E-03	6.E-03

Significant level: * 1%   * * 5%
The figures unter the parameters are standard errors

Table 11 shows estimation results of Tri-variate GARCH models. All parameters in conditional variance are significantly estimated. From this estimation, we take out the variance and covariance of estimated h_{it}.

Table 12. Volatility from Tri-variate GARCH

	2008	2007	Lehman
COV_LEJP_LEUS	1.51E-07	4.63E-08	6.48E-07
COV_LEJP_LUSJP	3.34E-07	1.83E-07	1.18E-06
COV_LEUS_LUSJP	-1.10E-07	-1.20E-08	-1.23E-07
VOL_LEJP	4.85E-07	2.45E-07	1.95E-06
VOL_LEUS	3.06E-07	6.20E-08	8.04E-07
VOL_LUSJP	5.49E-07	2.09E-07	1.34E-06

In Table12, covariances of each pair are shown in first three columns, and variances are in last three columns. During turbulent days, covariance and valiance are highest. This means volatility in those days is higher than other periods. Covariance between Euro/USD and USD/JPY is minus in all periods. This is consistent with the fact we have already confirmed in Table 4.

To clarify the volatility structure, we apply VAR model again to the estimated conditional variances. In this case, we just show the result of Granger Causality test in VAR model.

Table 13. Granger Causality test in Vector Auto Regression Model : Volatility

		2008	2007	Lehman
Dependent	Independent	Chi-sq	Chi-sq	Chi-sq
VOL_LEJP	VOL_LEUS	69.32*	38.57*	0.06
	VOL_LUSJP	9.62*	22.41*	2.08
	All	76.57*	55.04*	2.22
VOL_LEUS	VOL_LEJP	42.62*	18.91*	4.36
	VOL_LUSJP	31.74*	18.25*	9.58*
	All	58.03*	71.61*	12.15*
VOL_LUSJP	VOL_LEJP	24.75*	87.26*	2.18
	VOL_LEUS	47.7*	39.66*	0.44
	All	83.29*	106.83*	2.28

Significant level: * 1%   ** 5%

From Table 13, spillover of volatility among these three foreign exchange rate are clear in 2008 and 2007. Only one case we can find in Lehman shock days, USD/JPY volatility may affect EUR/USD volatility. This fact finding is consistent with our prediction in some part. US Dollar based foreign exchange volatility may lead other volatility in a turbulent market Lehman Brothers failure caused.

5. Summary

Special event may have significant effect on financial market. Announcement of some economic indicator is one of the events which have significant effect on financial market. In this paper, we pick up the Lehman Brothers shock to investigate what will happen in foreign exchange market.

It is predictable that stock market will suffer a big damage by this problem. But we do not have enough knowledge on the impact of this shock on foreign exchange market. There are so many paths of the impact from stock market to foreign exchange. If stock prices in Tokyo market go down, what will happen in foreign exchange market? Foreign investors may sell their stock, and withdraw their asset from Japan and transfer them to their countries. Through this action, Japanese Yen will depreciate. In actual market today, investors in foreign exchange market used to buy Japanese Yen when Japanese stock prices go down because investors take this tendency as increase of the risk in financial market and they want to sell US Dollar to avoid risk. With this trade, Japanese Yen appreciate with Japanese stock price depreciation. In this way, the relation between stock market and foreign exchange market is ambiguous. When we face this kind of event, we may have difficulties to invest our fund rationally, even for professional dealers.

US Dollar, Euro and Japanese Yen are most heavily traded financial asset in the world. If US Dollar depreciates against Euro and Japanese Yen, Euro against Japanese Yen must be changed. But we cannot predict whether Euro appreciates or not. This direction should be determined by the relative magnitude of the change of Euro and Japanese Yen's value against US Dollar. If Euro appreciates against US Dollar a lot and

Japanese Yen appreciates against US Dollar a bit. Then, Euro will appreciate against Japanese Yen through triangular arbitrage. At this moment, arbitrage opportunity might happen, but cannot last so long. Foreign exchange rates against US Dollar might change first, and then other rates will be determined through these series of arbitrage.

In this paper, we use ultra high frequent foreign exchange data to investigate the relations among US Dollar, Euro and Japanese Yen in turbulent market condition. Because of triangular arbitrage condition, stable relations among these currencies must exist. The more the market is getting turbulent, the more the arbitrage opportunities might exist. If US Dollar value moves a lot in a short time, then relative value between Euro and Japanese Yen must be unstable. Here, arbitrage opportunities occur. We suppose that the candidate of the source of turbulence of the market is unknown shock such as Lehman shock.

Just after the Lehman Brothers problem occurred, not only stock market but also foreign exchange market moved a lot. We take this opportunity to investigate the relations among these three most traded assets to explore whether market turbulence may yield arbitrage opportunities.

We found out that three foreign exchange rates are affecting each other in the long run. But in the turbulent period, this interdependency is getting weaker. The result from VEC model shows that the relations among three currencies are different especially for EUR/JPY. USD based rate did not affect on EUR/JPY in turbulent period, whereas USD based rate had clear effect on EUR/JPY during benchmark period. This finding indicates that more arbitrage opportunities occurred in EUR/JPY in turbulent period. With the VAR and Granger Causality, we found that relations in volume and orderflow are weaker in turbulent period. Volatility covariance is highest in turbulent period but the causality is weak in this period from t-GARCH model. All these results indicate that the possibility of appearance of arbitrage opportunities rises with market turbulence.

References

[1]   Admati,A., Pfeiderer, P., 1988 A Theory of Intraday Patterns: Volume and Price Variability, *Review of Financial Studies*, 1, 3-40.

[2]   Andersen,T., Bollerslev, T., 1996, Heterogeneous Information Arrivals and Returns Volatility Dynamics: Uncovering the Long-Run in High Frequency Rendements, NBER Working Paper No.5752.

[3]   Andersen,T., Bollerslev, T., 1998, Deutsche Mark-Dollar Volatility: Intraday Volatility Patterns, Macroeconomic Announcement and Longer Run Dependencies, *Journal of Finance*, 53, 219-265.

[4]   Bauwens,L., Omrane,W.B., and P.Giot, 2005, News Announcements, Market Activity and Volatility in the Euro/Dollar Foreign Exchange Market, *Journal of International Money and Finance*, 24, 1421-1443.

[5]   Bauwens,L., Rime,D., and G.Succarat, 2006, Exchange Rate Volatility and the Mixture of Distribution Hypothesis, *Empirical Economics*,30, 889-911.

[6]   Cai,J., Cheung,Y.L., Lee,R.S.K., and M.Melvin, 2001, Once in a Generation Yen Volatility in 1998: Fundamentals, Intervention and Order Flow, *Journal of International Money and Finance*, 20, 327-347.

[7]   Clark,P., 1973, A Subordinated Stochastic Process Model with Finite Variance for Speculative Prices, *Econometrica*, 41, 135-155.

[8]   Covrig,V., Melvin, M., 2002, Asymmetric Information and Price Discovery in the FX Market: Does Tokyo know more about Yen? *Journal of Empirical Finance*, 9, 271-285.

[9]   Danielsson,J., Payne, R., 2002, Real Trading Pattern and Prices in the Spot Foreign Exchange Market, *Journal of International Money and Finance*, 21, 203-222.

[10]   Degennaro,R., Shrieves, R., 1997, Public Information Releases, Private Information Arrival and Volatility in the Foreign Exchange Market, *Journal of Empirical Finance*, 4, 295-315.

[11]   Dominguez,K.M.E., Panthaki, F., 2006, What defines "News" in Foreign Exchange Markets? *Journal of International Money and Finance*, 25, 168-198.

[12]   Ehrmann,M., Fratzscher, M. 2005, Exchange Rates and Fundamentals: New Evidence from Real-Time Data, *Journal of International Money and Finance*, 24, 317-341.

[13]   Engle, R, F., Lin, W.L., and T.Ito, 1990, Meteor Showers or Heat Waves? Hetroskedastic Intra-daily Volatility in the Foreign Exchange market, *Econometrica*, 58, 525-542.

[14]   Evans,M, Lyons, R., 2002, Order Flow and Exchange Rate Dynamics, *Journal of Political Economy*, 110, 170-180.

[15]   Evans,M, Lyons, R., 2006, Understanding Order Flow, International Journal of Finance and Economics, 11, 3-23.

[16] Frommel,M., Alexander,M., and L.Menkhoff, 2008, Order Flows, News, and Exchange Rate Volatility, *Journal of International Money and Finance*, 27, 994-1012.

[17] Glosten,L., Milgrom, P., 1985, Bid Ask and Transaction Prices in a Specialist Market with Heterogeneously Informed Traders, *Journal of Financial Economics*, 13, 71-100.

[18] Ito, T., Lyons, R K., and M.T. Melvin, 1998, Is There Private Information in the FX Market? The Tokyo Experiment, *Journal of Finance*, LIII, 1111-1130.

[19] Ito, T., V. V. Roley, 1987, News from the U.S. and Japan: Which Moves the Yen/Dollar Exchange Rate? *Journal of Monetary Economics,* 19, 255-277.

[20] Ito, T., V. V. Roley, 1991, Intraday Yen/Dollar Exchange Rate Movements: News or Noise? *Journal of International Financial Markets, Institutions and Money*, 1, 1-31.

[21] Killeen,W.P., Lyons,R.K., and M.J.Moore, 2006, Fixed versus Flexible: Lessons from EMS order flow, *Journal of International Money and Finance*, 25, 551-579.

[22] Lamoureux,C.G., Lastrapes,W.D., Heteroscedasticity in Stock Return Data: Volume versus GARCH Effects, *Journal of Finance*, 45, 221-229.

[23] Lyons,R, 1995, Tests of Microstructural Hypotheses in the Foreign Exchange Market, *Journal of Financial Economics*, 39, 321-351.

[24] Lyons,R, 2001, The Microstructure Approach to Exchange Rates, MIT Press.

[25] Melvin,M, Yin, X., 2000, Public Information Arrival, Exchange Rate Volatility and Quote Frequency, *The Economic Journal*, 110, 644-661.

[26] Sager,M.J., Taylor, M.P., 2006, Under the Microscope: The Structure of the Foreign Exchange Market, *International Journal of Finance and Economics*, 11, 81-95.

[27] Susai,M., 2006, Empirical analysis on the volatility spillover among Northeast Asian stock markets with the effect of bilateral foreign exchange rate fluctuation, *Proceedings of the 18th Asia Pacific International Conference on Accounting Issues*, Maui, Hawaii.

[28] Susai,M., 2008, Tokyo or New York:Which Drives East Asian Stock Markets? In M.Susai, H.Okada (eds.,), *Empirical Study on Asian Financial Markets*, Kyushu University Press, 1-39.

Chapter 2

The Asymmetric Contagion from the U.S. Stock Market around the Subprime Crisis

Chien-Chung Nieh

Professor of Department of Banking and Finance,
Tamkang University, Taipei, Taiwan.

Yu-Sheng Kao

Ph.D. student of Department of Banking and Finance,
Tamkang University, Taipei, Taiwan.

Chao-Hsiang Yang

Ph.D. student of Department of Banking and Finance,
Tamkang University, Taipei, Taiwan

Abstract

The Enders and Siklos (2001) asymmetric threshold co-integration model was applied to examine the long-term asymmetric equilibrium relationships between the U.S. and three major European and the U.S. and three major Latin American stock markets around the subprime mortgage crisis. First, from the major empirical results of our research, we have found that partially asymmetric co-integration relationships between the U.S. and European and the U.S. and Latin American stock markets has increased during the crisis, which partly supports the "contagion effect" and partly supports the "interdependence effect" of the international stock markets, which was proposed by Forbes and Rigobon (2001). Hence, the event of the subprime mortgage crisis enhanced partial co-movement between the U.S. and European and the U.S. and Latin American stock markets, except the Brazil stock market, which demonstrated only the interdependence effect with the S&P 500 index. Therefore, if the investors in these countries want to diversify risks by utilizing the investment portfolios of the stock markets in the U.S. and their own countries, they should cautiously consider the correlations of the categories of industries before making any investment during the subprime mortgage crisis. The subprime mortgage crisis, which is different from previous financial crises in emerging markets, reveals that the financial linkage of a country to the U.S. markets determines the degrees of contagion effects.

1. Introduction and Literature Review

Because the financial markets are globalized and deregulated all over the world, an economic shock from one country often impacts the countries in the same region or countries in other regions when a regional or a global economic crisis takes place. Exogenous events and contagion are the issues that researchers have been interested in. The recent crisis- contagion theory is ardently discussed by the authorities of governments and scholars. The collapse of the U.S. stock market in 1987, the Mexico peso crisis in 1994, the Asian Financial Crisis in 1997, and the Russian financial crisis in 1998 all resulted in the decline of the stock markets of other countries in the same region. The co-movement in the international stock markets weakens the effect of risk diversification for investors who utilize international security portfolios.

The U.S. is the largest economic entity and importer of goods in the world. Theoretically, the impact of an economic shock in the U.S. would affect a broader region. In March 2007, there was a financial crisis in the New Century Financial Corp., which was the second largest mortgage company. It was involved in the practice of illegal lending, which ignited the subprime mortgage crisis (Gorton, 2008) which affected the financial world. It led to the financial turmoil in the U.S. and Europe. The Wall Street giants suffered severe loss. Bear Stearns and Merrill Lynch were merged by other banks, Lehman Brothers filed a bankruptcy, and Fannie Mae, Freddie Mac, and AIG all suffered huge loss due to their investment in subprime debts. Fed poured more than 100 billion dollars into the financial market to purchase the non-performing loans. The U.S. Congress also passed the Emergency

Economic Stabilization Act (EESA), which included 700 billion dollars' Troubled Asset Relief Program (TARP), on October 4, 2008. In Europe, bankruptcies were filed in Belgium, the U.K., Germany, and Iceland. There was even a "government bankruptcy" in Iceland, which had been a term unheard of in the history.

The subprime mortgage crisis also hit the real output in the economy. Corporate bankruptcies accompanied by unemployment and capital expenditure cuts led to the decline in every country in consumption, investment, import, and export. The U.S., East Europe, Eurozone and part of Asia all suffered a recession in the fourth quarter in 2008. The scholars thought the chain reactions incurred by the subprime mortgage crisis had never been seen since the Great Depression. The financial institutions and investors invested in subprime products lost a lot of money. Hence, the liquidity of the financial markets was decreasing severely. The financial institutions needed capital injections from their governments. The major industrial countries made their efforts and coordinated their policies to rescue the financial disaster.

The World Bank has given contagion three definitions, namely, a broad definition, a restrictive definition, and a very restrictive definition. The broad definition means that contagion is the cross-country transmission of shocks or the general cross-country spillover effects; contagion does not need to be related to crises. The restrictive definition means that contagion is the transmission of shocks to other countries or the cross-country correlation, beyond any fundamental link among the countries and beyond common shocks. This definition is usually referred to as excess co-movement, commonly explained by herding behavior. The very restrictive definition means that contagion occurs when cross-country correlations increase during "crisis times" relative to correlations during "tranquil times." In literature, a crisis contagion theory explains that if there is co-movement or a common trend between different markets, then a shock in one market will transmit to another market. But scholars have a different definition of contagion. Dornbusch *et al.* (2000) defined contagion as a significant increase in cross market linkages after a shock to an individual country, as measured by the degree to which asset prices or financial flows moved together across markets relative to this co-movement in tranquil times. Forbes and Rigobon (2001) divided how the shocks were propagated into two groups of theories: crisis-contingent and non-crisis-contingent theories. Crisis-contingent theories are those that explain why transmission mechanisms change during a crisis, and therefore why cross-market linkages increase after a shock. Non-crisis-contingent theories assume that transmission mechanisms are the same during a crisis or at more stable periods, and therefore cross-market linkages do not increase after a shock.

In empirical literature, four different methodologies have been utilized to measure how shocks are transmitted internationally: cross-market correlation coefficients, ARCH or GARCH frameworks, co-integration techniques, and direct estimation of specific transmission mechanisms by using the Probit model.

King and Wadhwani (1990) first used the correlation approach and found that cross-market correlations increased significantly among the U.S., the U.K., and Japan after the U.S. stock market collapse in October 1987. Kasa (1992) showed the presence of a single common trend among the stock markets in the U.S., the U.K., Germany, Canada, and Japan. Lee and Kim (1993) found that international stock markets had become more interrelated after the October 1987 U.S. stock market collapse. The strengthening co-movement among international stock markets continued for a longer period after the collapse. Cha and Oh (2000) showed evidence that the links between the developed markets and the Asian emerging markets began to increase after the U.S. stock market collapse in 1987. The links had significantly intensified since the Asian Financial Crisis in 1997.

Forbes and Rigobon (2002) argued that tests for contagion based on cross-market correlation coefficients were problematic due to the bias introduced by changing volatility in market return (heteroskedasticity). They showed that correlation coefficients were conditional on market volatility. Under the assumption of no omitted variables or endogeneity, it is possible to adjust this bias. By using this adjustment, there was virtually no increase in unconditional correlation coefficients (i.e., no contagion) during the 1997 Asian Financial Crisis, 1994 Mexican devaluation, and 1987 U.S. stock market collapse. There was a high level of market co-movement, which they called interdependence, in all periods. Caporale *et al.* (2005) modeled the conditional variance by the application of both heteroskedasticity and endogeneity biases and invented a common shock to deal with the omitted variable problem. They found the existence of contagion within the stock markets in Hong Kong, Japan, South Korea, Singapore, Taiwan, and Malaysia during the 1997 Asian Financial Crisis. The findings were consistent with the crisis-contingent theories of stock market linkages.

Hamao *et al.* (1990) utilized the GARCH model and pointed out that the volatility spillovers of the stock indices from New York to Tokyo, London to Tokyo, and New York to London after the U.S. stock market collapse in 1987 were observed. Many researchers considered significant increases of correlation or co-movement of the stock markets were the indicators of a contagion effect. Eun and Shim (1989) used the VAR model and found that a substantial amount of multi-lateral interaction existed among the international stock markets. Innovations in the U.S. were rapidly transmitted to other markets in a clearly recognizable fashion, whereas no single foreign market could significantly impact the movement of the U.S. stock market. Ghosh (1999) utilized the theory of co-integration to investigate which Asian developing markets were moved by the markets of Japan and the U.S. He suggested that some countries were dominated by the U.S., some were dominated by Japan, and the remaining countries were dominated by neither. Sheng and Tu (2000) found that co-integration did not exist in the eleven Asian stock markets and U.S. stock markets before the 1997 Asian Financial Crisis, but it did during the financial crisis, which demonstrated a contagion effect. If co-integration exists between international stock markets, there will be a common trend. However, the problems of "nonlinear" or "asymmetric" characteristics are not considered in the traditional co-integration model. Li and Lam (1995), Koutmos (1998), and Chiang (2001) pointed out that co-integration between stock markets was asymmetric; therefore, asymmetric adjustments could exist in an upward status (positive impact) or a downward status (negative impact). How did the phenomenon influence the transmission effect of the stock markets? Did different correlations, co-movement, interdependence, or contagion effects exist in bull markets or bear markets? These issues were seldom discussed in previous literature; therefore, we decided to explore these problems by the asymmetric threshold co-integration model.

What is the impact of the U.S. stock market collapse on the global stock markets during the subprime mortgage crisis? Is co-integration strengthened during the financial disaster? The issue of the contagion effect in some countries in Europe and Latin America, which we have selected for this paper, is carefully examined.

The KSS's nonlinear ESTAR unit root test and the asymmetric threshold co-integration model, which we employed to investigate the contagion effect, will be discussed in Section 2. The data and empirical results will be shown in Section 3. The conclusions will be presented in Section 4.

2. Methodologies

2.1 *Advanced Nonlinear ESTAR Unit root test*

Recently, there is a growing consensus that stock market price indices might be non-linear and that the conventional unit root test has lower power in detecting its mean reverting (stationary) tendency. As such, this study employs a newly developed non-linear stationary test advanced by Kapetanios *et al.* (2003) to determine if the stock market indices of this paper are non-linear stationary.

The KSS nonlinear stationary test is based on detecting the presence of non-stationarity against nonlinear but a globally stationary exponential smooth transition autoregressive model (ESTAR) process:

$$\Delta Y_t = \theta Y_{t-1}[1 - \exp(-\gamma Y_{t-1}^2)] + v_t \tag{1}$$

where Y_t is the data series of variable considered, v_t is an i.i.d. error with a zero mean and constant variance, and $\gamma \geq 0$ is known as the transition parameter or smooth parameter of the ESTAR model that governs the speed of transition. We are now interested in testing the null hypothesis of $\gamma = 0$ against the alternative of $\gamma > 0$. Under the null hypothesis, Y_t follows a linear unit root process, whereas it's a nonlinear stationary ESTAR process under alternative. However, the parameter θ isn't identified under the null hypothesis. Kapetanios *et al.* (2003) follow Luukkonen *et al.* (1988) to compute a first-order Taylor series approximation to the $[1 - \exp(-\gamma Y_{t-1}^2)]$ under the null of $\gamma = 0$, and approximate Equations (1) by the following auxiliary regression:

$$\Delta Y_t = \alpha + \delta Y_{t-1}^3 + \sum_{I=1}^{P-1} \beta_i \Delta Y_{t-d} + v_t, \qquad t = 1, 2, \ldots\ldots, T \qquad (2)$$

Then, the null hypothesis and alternative hypothesis are expressed as $\delta = 0$ (non stationarity) against $\delta < 0$ (nonlinear stationarity).

2.2 Threshold Co-integration and Asymmetric Adjustment

In order to examine the "asymmetric contagion effect" from the U.S. to three major European and the U.S. to three major Latin American stock markets during the subprime mortgage crisis, we employed the Enders and Granger (1998) and Enders and Siklos (2001) method of asymmetric threshold co-integration. Conventional tests for the unit root and co-integration, whether proposed by Engle and Granger (1987) or Johansen (1988), are misspecified when the adjustment process of the one-period lagged error term is asymmetric. The Enders and Siklos (2001) technique extended the Engle and Granger (1987) framework to test non-linear co-integration (also see Enders and Granger, 1998). In our analysis of the contagion effect from the U.S. stock markets to three major European and three major Latin American stock markets around the subprime mortgage crisis, we employed the Enders and Siklos (2001) test for threshold co-integration. In this study we used the daily observations; therefore, we considered $Y_{i,t}$ was the logarithm of three European and three Latin American stock price indices on period t, and X_{t-1} was the logarithm of the U.S. stock price index on period $t-1$ because we had to consider the factor of time lag of the trading day of the U.S. stock markets and the European stock markets (see Eun and

Shim, 1989; Liu *et al.*, 1998)[1].   Let the long-term equilibrium relationship be:

$$Y_{i,t} = \eta_0 + \eta_1 X_{t-1} + \varepsilon_t \qquad i = 1, 2 \ldots \ldots, 6 \qquad (3)$$

Where $i = 1, \ldots, 6$, ε_t measures the estimated residuals from the estimated co-integration relationship between Y_t and X_{t-1}, respectively, both integration of order 1 (i.e. $I(1)$) if the two series are co-integrated; otherwise, the test rejects the null hypothesis of no co-integration. Enders and Siklos (2001) modifies ε_t to allow for two types of asymmetric error corrections based on a co-integrating relationship as depicted in Equation (3). First, ε_t is estimated via OLS (3).   Next, the residuals ε_t, are used in:

$$\Delta\varepsilon_t = I_t \rho_1 \varepsilon_{t-1} + (1 - I_t)\rho_2 \varepsilon_{t-1} + \sum_{i=1}^{p-1} \beta_i \Delta\varepsilon_{t-i} + \zeta_t \qquad (4)$$

where $I_t = [T_t, M_t]$, such that:

$$T_t = \begin{cases} 1 & \text{if } \varepsilon_{t-1} \geq c \\ 0 & \text{if } \varepsilon_{t-1} < c \end{cases} \qquad (5a)$$

$$M_t = \begin{cases} 1 & \text{if } \Delta\varepsilon_{t-1} \geq r \\ 0 & \text{if } \Delta\varepsilon_{t-1} < r \end{cases} \qquad (5b)$$

where $I_t [T_t, M_t]$ is the Heaviside indicator function, ζ_t is the residual of the white-noise disturbance and c and r denote the unknown threshold values.   Equations (4) and (5a) represent the threshold autoregressive model (TAR) where the indicator function T_t depends on the previous period's ε_{t-1}.   Equations (4) and (5b) represent the Momentum threshold autoregressive model (M-TAR).   Enders and Granger (1998) pointed out the M-TAR model was especially valuable when adjustment was asymmetric such that the series exhibited more "momentum" in one direction than the other.

In the TAR model, the adjustment is modeled by $\rho_1 \varepsilon_{t-1}$ that $T_t = 1$ when the residual according to (5a) is above the threshold value c and by

---

[1] In this study, the sample of trading day does not have one day lag when we examine the asymmetric co-integration relationship between the U.S. and Latin American stock markets.

the term $\rho_2\varepsilon_{t-1}$ that $T_t = 0$ when the residual is below the threshold value. In the M-TAR model, the adjustment is modeled by $\rho_1\varepsilon_{t-1}$ that $M_t = 1$ when the residual according to (5b) is above the threshold value r and by the term $\rho_2\varepsilon_{t-1}$ that $M_t = 0$ when the residual is below the threshold value. The threshold value is endogenously determined by using the Chan's (1993) grid search method to find the consistent estimate of the threshold. This method arranges the values, {ε_t and $\Delta\varepsilon_t$}, in an ascending order and excludes the smallest and largest 15 percent, and the consistent estimate of the threshold is the parameter that yields the smallest residual sum squares (RSS) over the remaining 70 percent. Enders and Granger (1998) and Enders and Siklos (2001) both indicated in either case, under the null hypothesis of no convergence, the F-statistic for the null hypothesis $H_0 : \rho_1 = \rho_2 = 0$ had a nonstandard distribution. Enders and Granger (1998) also indicated that if the series was stationary, the least squares estimates of ρ_1 and ρ_2 had an asymptotic multivariate normal distribution. We tested the null hypothesis $H_0 : \rho_1 = \rho_2 = 0$ for the co-integration relationship, and rejection implied the existence of co-integration relationship between two variables. If the null hypothesis of no co-integration was rejected, it would enable us to proceed with a further test for symmetric adjustment of the null hypothesis, which was $H_0 : \rho_1 = \rho_2$. We proceeded with the asymmetric threshold co-integration test and symmetric adjustment test by using the usual standard F-statistic.

The TAR model interprets departures from the equilibrium as creating forces to restore the long-run relationship if the size of the disequilibrium is larger than some threshold. The MTAR model can capture an accumulation of changes in the disequilibrium relationship between the U.S. stock market and the European and the U.S. and Latin American stock markets below and above the threshold followed by a sharp movement back to the equilibrium position.

3. Data and Empirical Results

This research is conducted by using the basis of the U.S., three major European, and three major Latin American stock market indices. In this study, we chose the S&P 500 index as the sample of the U.S. stock market indices. The trade stocks in the S&P 500 index include the top

500 enterprises in the New York Stock Exchange (NYSE) and the American Stock Exchange (AMEX). The reason why the S&P 500 index was chosen was because the total market value of the S&P 500 index dominated over 80% of the total value of NYSE. In addition, after taking factors such as liquidity and industrial representation into consideration, we believed that this index could reflect the conditions of the capital markets, the security markets, and the economy of the U.S more validly than the Dow Jones index. The European and Latin American stock market indices include the FTSE 100 index (U.K.), DAX index (Germany), CAC 40 index (France), IPC index (Mexico), MERVAL index (Argentina), and IBOVESPA index (Brazil), and all observations are taken logarithm. The entire sample period was from 2004/1/2 to 2009/9/25 for a total of 1304 daily observations which were obtained for each variable[2]. The FTSE 100 index, DAX index, and CAC 40 index are the three major stock markets in Europe. The IPC index, MERVAL index, and IBOVESPA index are the three stock markets with the maximum market volumes in Latin America. Chen *et al.* (2002) indicated the market capitalization in Mexico, Argentina, and Brazil was US$ 91,746 million, US$ 45,332 million, and US$ 160,887 million in 1998, respectively. The values of stocks traded were US$ 33,841 million, US$ 15,078 million, and US$ 146,594 million, which ranked as the top three in Latin America.

Table 1 represents the summary statistics for all the series and Table 2 represents the correlation coefficients between the U.S. and European and the U.S. and Latin American stock market indices around the subprime mortgage crisis and in all sample periods. Since there is still no consensus on the start date for the subprime mortgage crisis, it is not easy to determine an exact date. In general, some scholars (see Gorton, 2008) consider the outburst of the financial crisis of the New Century Financial Corp. as the beginning of the crisis. Therefore we used the date on which the trading of stock of New Century Financial Corp. was

---

[2] Trading days and closing days were different in various stock markets; therefore, if one market did not have any transaction on a particular day, we would delete the data in other markets on the same day. We only kept the data of synchronized trading days in all stock markets. Hamao *et al.* (1990) pointed out that discarding the data of non-synchronized trading days would not affect the accuracy of the empirical results.

terminated in NYSE, that is, 2007/3/13, as the cutting point. Thus, the period of "pre subprime mortgage crisis" was defined as the period from 2004/1/2 to 2007/3/13 and the period of "during the subprime mortgage crisis" was defined as the period from 2007/3/14 to 2009/9/25.

Table 1. Summary Statistics for return on Stock indices (2004/1/2~2009/9/25)

	S&P 500	FTSE 100	DAX	CAC 40	IPC	MERVAL	IBOVESPA
Mean	-0.00457	0.00916	0.0252	0.00298	0.0907	0.0464	0.0759
Max.	10.4236	11.1112	13.4627	13.3048	11.1115	10.4316	15.4728
Min.	-9.4695	-9.2646	-7.7391	-9.4715	-7.2661	-12.9516	-12.0961
Std. Dev	1.4487	1.3873	1.5257	1.5371	1,6241	2.1197	2.1761
Skewness	-0.2670*	0.1857*	0.4548*	0.3892*	0.2686*	-0.6569***	0.0666
Kurtosis	13.9199***	14.5732***	13.9090***	14.1886***	7.8147***	7.7990***	8.0790***
J-B	6489.41***	7279.23***	6505.90***	6829.32***	1274.24***	1344.07***	1401.51***
L-B Q(24)	132.72***	71.019***	20.413	57.757***	39.299**	42.436**	47.175***
	(0.000)	(0.000)	(0.673)	(0.000)	(0.025)	(0.012)	(0.003)

Notes: 1. *, ** and *** denote significance at 10%, 5% and 1% significance level, respectively.
2. J-B (Jarque-Bera) is the statistic of the normal test.

Table 2. The Correlation coefficient of return between S&P 500 index and the other stock markets

	(1) Entire period	(2) Pre-subprime crisis	(3) During-subprime crisis
FTSE 100	0.5847	0.4426	0.6093
DAX	0.6193	0.4739	0.6564
CAC 40	0.5932	0.4595	0.6207
IPC	0.7485	0.6162	0.8128
MERVAL	0.5912	0.3948	0.6959
IBOVESPA	0.7301	0.6158	0.7981
Average	0.6445	0.5005	0.6989

Note: The periods and sample sizes for entire period, Pre-subprime mortgage crisis and During-subprime mortgage crisis are (2004/1/2~2009/ 9/25, N =1304), (2004/1/2~2007/3/13, N =726) and (2007/3/14~2009/9/25, N =578), respectively.

The results in Table 2 show that the correlation coefficients increased between the U.S. and European and the U.S. and Latin American stock market indices during the subprime mortgage crisis, the result supported the crisis-contagion theory by Dornbusch *et al.* (2000) and Forbes and Rigobon (2001). The results of the three unit root tests, ADF, PP, and KPSS, are summarized in Table 3, which shows that the null hypothesis of non-stationarity can not be rejected for any levels of the series. After the first difference, the null is rejected at the 1% significance level for all the series. Therefore, we conclude that all the variables are the $I(1)$ type series at the 1% significance level. Table 4 represents the results of the KSS's (2003) nonlinear ESTAR unit root test, which shows that variables of all stock market indices in this study are $I(1)$ series at the 1% significance level.

Table 3. Results of Various Unit Root Tests

	Level			First difference		
	ADF	PP	KPSS	ADF	PP	KPSS
S&P 500	-1.8636 (6)	-1.9858	5.7133***	-21.9466 (5)***	-52.9389***	0.1855
FTSE 100	-1.3481 (7)	-1.4995	5.1729***	-22.7124 (5)***	-52.4000***	0.1343
DAX	-1.5277 (7)	-1.5267	5.2263***	-22.0575 (5)***	-49.5223***	0.1280
CAC 40	-1.8329 (7)	-1.8410	3.4085***	-23.1064 (5)***	-50.3363***	0.2699
IPC	-0.6503 (6)	-0.5449	31.7719***	-20.7821 (5)***	-45.7524***	0.1315
MERVAL	-1.1011 (8)	-0.9241	22.3167***	-22.8725 (3)***	-46.7779***	0.2014
IBOVESPA	-1.0374 (9)	-0.8825	20.5478***	-21.2697 (5)***	-48.7403***	0.0809

Notes: 1. *, ** and *** denote significance at the 10%, 5% and 1% significance level, respectively; the numbers in the parentheses are the appropriate lag-lengths selected by minimizing AIC.
2. The critical value for the 10%, 5% and 1% significance level of ADF, PP and KPSS are (-2.567894, -2.863559, -3.435176), (-2.567891, -2.863552, -3.435161) and (0.3470, 0.4630, 0.7390).
3. The null hypothesis of ADF and PP are non-stationary (unit root); the null hypothesis of KPSS is stationary (non unit root).

The entire period was divided into two parts, the period of "pre subprime mortgage crisis," and the period "during the subprime mortgage crisis". Table 5 represents the results of the Engle-Granger co-integration relationships between the U.S. and European and the U.S. and Latin American stock market indices in the entire period 〈Table 5-(1)〉, the period of pre-subprime mortgage crisis〈Table 5-(2)〉, and the period of during-subprime mortgage crisis〈Table 5-(3)〉, and it shows the null hypothesis of no co-integration in Table 5. In Table 5-(1), the results of the Engle-Granger ADF statistics show that there are no co-integration relationships between the S&P 500 Index and these stock markets at the 10 % significance level in the entire period. In Table 5-(2), the results show that there is only co-integration relationship between the S&P 500 Index and IPC index at the 5% significance level in the period of pre-subprime mortgage crisis. In Table 5-(3), the results show that there is only co-integration relationship between the S&P 500 Index and DAX index at the 1% significance level in the period of during-subprime mortgage crisis. The results in Table 5 show that there is significant increase in the co-integration relationship between the S&P 500 Index and DAX index around the subprime mortgage crisis; this result is not consistent with the results in Table 2, and it does not support the crisis-contagion theory by Dornbusch *et al.* (2000) and Forbes and Rigobon (2001).

Table 4. Results of the Nonlinear Unit Root Test – KSS Test

	t Statistics on $\hat{\delta}$	
	Level	First difference
S&P 500	-1.1821(2)	-19.1415(1)***
FTSE 100	-1.4900(2)	-17.2011(1)***
DAX	-1.4576(0)	-17.2963(0)***
CAC40	-1.1373(1)	-17.5471(2)***
IPC	-1.7207(1)	-18.4324(1)***
MERVAL	-1.6473(0)	-16.6389(2)***
IBOVESPA	-0.9944(1)	-19.7016(1)***

Notes: 1. The numbers in the parentheses are the appropriate lag-lengths selected by minimize AIC.
2. The simulated critical value for different Ks were tabulated in Kapetanios *et al.* (2003).
3. *, ** and *** denote significance at the 10%, 5% and 1% significance level, respectively.

Enders and Granger (1998) and Enders and Siklos (2001) proposed two models for the threshold co-integration test, namely, the TAR model and the M-TAR model[3]. This study adopts the M-TAR model. Table 6 represents the results of our estimation of the threshold co-integration relationships between the U.S. and European and the U.S. and Latin American stock market indices in the entire period ⟨ Table 6-(1) ⟩ , the period of pre-subprime mortgage crisis ⟨ Table 6-(2) ⟩ , and the period of during-subprime mortgage crisis ⟨ Table 6-(3) ⟩ , and it shows the null hypothesis of no co-integration (F_C) and symmetric adjustment (F_A) in Table 6. In Table 6-(1), the F_C statistics rejected the null hypothesis at the 1% significant level and the F_A statistics rejected the null at the 10% level in the entire period. Both F_C and F_A demonstrate the relationships of asymmetric co-integration between the S&P 500 index and all of the European and Latin American stock market indices in the entire period. Table 6-(2) and Table 6-(3) represent the results of the threshold co-integration relationship tests around the subprime mortgage crisis. In Table 6-(2), both F_C and F_A demonstrate the relationships of asymmetric co-integration between the S&P 500 index and CAC 40 index, IPC index in the period of pre-subprime mortgage crisis. In Table 6-(3), both F_C and F_A demonstrate the relationships of asymmetric co-integration between the S&P 500 index and all of the European and Latin American stock market indices during-subprime mortgage crisis. By further comparisons of the F_C statistics in Table 6-(2) and Table 6-(3), we have found that the co-integration relationships have significantly increased after the shock of the subprime mortgage crisis between the S&P 500 index and FTSE 100 index, DAX index, CAC 40 index, IPC index and MERVAL index. The result shows that there is a "contagion effect" between the S&P 500 index and FTSE 100 index, DAX index, CAC 40 index, IPC index and MERVAL index, but there is only an "interdependence effect" between the S&P 500 index and IBOVESPA index. Forbes and Rigobon (2001) defined the contagion of the

---

[3] Enders and Granger (1998) believed that when asymmetrical adjustments occurred in the data series, the determination of the Heaviside indicator function might also be decided by the first difference value of error correction term on period t-$1(\Delta\varepsilon_{t-1})$. Boucher (2007) pointed out that the speed of convergence of parameter estimation by using the M-TAR model would be faster than that of the TAR model.

international stock markets as a significant increase in cross market linkages or co-movement between one market and others after a shock or during a crisis, and our results supported the "contagion effect" between the S&P 500 index of U.S. stock markets and some of the stock markets in the surveyed countries.

Moreover, by further comparisons of the F_A statistics in Table 6-(2) and Table 6-(3), we have found that the asymmetry in the co-integration relationships has also significantly increased after the crisis between the S&P 500 index and all of the European and Latin American stock market indices. The result shows that the subprime mortgage crisis induced quick transmission of massive negative information among many stock markets. These lead to higher risk aversion for international investors.

According to the empirical results, the order of the ranks of the stock market co-integration relationship between the above-mentioned stock markets and the S&P 500 index is as follows: CAC 40 index, FTSE 100 index, DAX index, MERVAL index, IPC index and IBOVESPA index.

This can be explained with the fact that the financial markets of France, U.K. and Germany are advanced markets and have had more linkage with the U.S. financial markets. Whereas the financial markets of Argentina, Mexico, and Brazil are emerging markets and have less linkage with the U.S. financial markets.

Table 5. Results of the Engle-Granger test for Co-integration between S&P 500 index and the other stock markets

	(1) Entire period	(2) Pre-subprime crisis	(3) During-subprime crisis	Co-integration
FTSE 100	-1.992	-2.327	-2.968	increase
DAX	-1.073	-2.626	-4.091***	increase
CAC 40	-2.334	-2.363	-2.268	decrease
IPC	-1.364	-3.684**	-1.670	decrease
MERVAL	-1.231	-2.857	-1.138	decrease
IBOVESPA	-0.300	-2.451	-1.648	decrease

Notes: 1. The lag-length of difference Ks selected by minimizing AIC.

2. The critical values of ADF Statistics are taken from Engle and Yoo (1987).

3. *, ** and *** denote significance at the 10%, 5% and 1% significance level, respectively.

4. The periods and sample sizes for entire period, Pre-subprime mortgage crisis and During-subprime mortgage crisis are (2004/1/2~2009/ 9/25, N =1304), (2004/1/2~ 2007/3/13, N =726) and (2007/3/14~2009/9/25, N =578), respectively.

Table 6. Results of the Ender and Siklos test for Threshold Co-integration between S&P 500 index and the other stock markets

	(1) Entire period			(2) Pre-subprime crisis			(3) During-subprime crisis			Co-integration	Asymmetric	Contagion? Y/N
	F_C	F_A	r	F_C	F_A	r	F_C	F_A	r			
FTSE100	109.455***	15.836***	0.0073	53.354***	1.030	0.00663	159.484***	19.940***	-0.00831	increase	increase	Y
DAX	97.956***	10.368***	0.01478	54.435***	1.977	0.00933	128.737***	16.167***	0.00587	increase	increase	Y
CAC40	146.796***	11.408***	0.01457	60.601***	4.142**	-0.00564	187.742***	17.432***	-0.00765	increase	increase	Y
IPC	38.140***	4.891**	-0.0138	18.068***	4.171**	0.01666	50.140***	9.307***	-0.01528	increase	increase	Y
MERVAL	49.472***	7.481***	0.01973	17.449***	1.641	0.01989	77.752***	4.822**	-0.01108	increase	increase	Y
IBOVESPA	38.593***	3.122*	0.02025	52.893***	1.707	0.02623	44.137***	7.728***	-0.02053	decrease	increase	N

Notes: 1. The lag-length of difference Ks selected by minimizing AIC; r is the estimated threshold value.

2. F_C and F_A denote the F-statistics for the null hypothesis of no co-integration and symmetric adjustment. Critical values are taken from Enders and Siklos (2001).

3. *, ** and *** denote significance at the 10%, 5% and 1% significance level, respectively.

4. The periods and sample sizes for entire period, Pre-subprime mortgage crisis and During-subprime mortgage crisis are (2004/1/2~2009/ 9/25, N =1304), (2004/1/2~2007/3/13, N =726) and (2007/3/14~2009/9/25, N =578), respectively.

The contagion effects on European markets were stronger than those on Latin American markets. In the past, most of the financial crises originated from the countries, which were considered to be emerging markets, with a lot of foreign debt, weak financial institutions, and unsound financial supervisory systems. The neighboring countries were apt to be influenced because they are near the origin of a financial crisis geographically. However, the subprime mortgage crisis was due to the huge losses of credit derivatives in the U.S. market. It originated from the most advanced country and no one expected this could happen. Surprisingly, the most severely influenced markets were not the neighboring Latin American markets. Therefore, the extent of financial linkage with the U.S. market might be the explanatory factor of strength of the contagion effect. Because many financial institutions and investors held subprime mortgage securities in the U.K., France and Germany, it was reasonable that the contagion effects were more significant in the European markets than in the Latin American markets. In short, the origin and impact of the subprime mortgage crisis are different from those of the financial crises in emerging markets.

4. Conclusions

The crisis contagion theory states that exogenous shocks are transmitted to many countries through transmission mechanisms. This effect leads to co-movement of stock markets. Dornbusch *et al.* (2000) and Forbes and Rigobon (2001) pointed out that contagion effects existed when negative impacts occurred.

Although there were many empirical works on international stock market contagion in the past, the contagion effect caused by the subprime mortgage crisis was quite different from previous crises. For example, during the collapse of the U.S. stock market in 1987, there were more financial regulations and less derivative trading. Moreover, the Mexico peso crisis in 1994, the Asian financial crisis in 1997, and the Russian financial crisis in 1998 were all regional crises in emerging markets. A regional crisis only had contagion effects in a particular area.

Apparently, the impact of the subprime mortgage crisis is greater than the above events.

Co-integration analysis is widely used to investigate whether or not the long-term equilibrium between stock markets is changed when a financial crisis happens. If the equilibrium relationship changes, the contagion effect occurs. However, the traditional co-integration analysis ignores the characteristics of asymmetric adjustment in stock markets (Li and Lam, 1995; Koutmos, 1998; Sarantis, 2001; Chiang, 2001). Therefore, this paper employed the Enders and Siklos (2001) asymmetric threshold co-integration model which allows asymmetric adjustment when analyzing stock market relationships. We tested the long-term equilibrium relationship between the U.S. and U.K., Germany, France, Mexico, Argentina, and Brazil stock markets.

The co-integration relationship between stock markets represents market co-movement. In this study, we anticipated contagion effects among international stock markets would lead to co-integration between the U.S. and European and the U.S. and Latin American stock markets. However, the results of the Engle-Granger ADF co-integration test did not indicate co-integration relationships between the U.S. and the six stock markets. These results were not consistent with the correlation analysis because the correlation coefficients between the U.S. and the six stock markets increased. In addition, these results were different from previous empirical studies. Our assumption could not be verified by traditional co-integration methods. However, the test results of the Enders and Siklos asymmetric threshold co-integration model did indicate that co-integration relationship increased. Therefore, the asymmetric threshold co-integration model is a better model to analyze the dynamic stock market relationships.

There are three major findings in this research. First, the empirical results support previous research. We find that co-integration between the S&P 500 index and the U.K., Germany, France, Mexico, and Argentina stock markets increases. Only co-integration between the S&P 500 index and Brazil stock market decreases. The information demonstrates that the subprime mortgage crisis in the U.S. had a contagion effect on international stock markets. Furthermore, when comparing the asymmetric adjustment in stock markets, the influence of good news and bad news in the U.S. market increased significantly during the crisis (asymmetric threshold co-integration). It was more likely that the transmission of massive negative information resulted in higher risk aversion for international investors.

Our second finding differs from previous literature. Previous works on financial crises found that most crises originated from emerging markets. (Aggarwal *et al.*, 1999; Collins and Biekpe, 2003; Dungey *et al.*, 2006) The neighboring countries were easily affected because they are geographically close to the origin of the financial crisis. Nevertheless, the subprime mortgage crisis was not from an emerging market. In addition, the contagion effect of the three European countries was more significant than that of the three Latin American countries. It was contrary to our anticipation that Latin American countries would be affected severely. The possible explanation was that the degree of financial linkage with the U.S. market contributed to the strength of the contagion effect. Since the U.K., Germany, and France markets were globalized and deregulated markets, they were affected notably. While the Mexico, Argentina, and Brazil markets were less globalized and less deregulated, they were affected moderately. Unlike a financial crisis of an emerging market, the subprime mortgage crisis caused quite different contagion effects which were explored in this research.

Thirdly, the subprime mortgage crisis has weakened international portfolio diversification. International investors can not diversify their risks by investing in the European and Latin American stock markets during the crisis. It is likely that if a world financial center is in trouble, global investors will be unavoidably influenced.

References

[1] Aggarwal, C., Inclan, C., and Leal, R., 1999, "Volatility in emerging stock markets," *Journal of Financial and Quantitative Analysis*, 4, 33-55.

[2] Boucher, C., 2007, "Asymmetric Adjustment of Stock Prices to their Fundamental Value and the Predictability of US Stock Returns," *Economic Letters*, 95, 339-347.

[3] Caporale, G.M., Cipollini, A., and Spagnolo, N., 2005, "Testing for Contagion: A Conditional Correlation Analysis," *Journal of Empirical Finance*, 12, 476-489.

38   C. Nieh, Y. Kao & C. Yang

[4] Cha, B. and Oh, S., 2000, "The Relationship between Developed Equity Markets and the Pacific Basin's Emerging Equity Markets," *International Review of Economics and Finance*, 9, 299–322.

[5] Chan, K. S., 1993, "Consistency and Limiting Distribution of the Least Squares Estimator of a Threshold Autoregressive Model," *The Annals of Statistics*, 21, 520-533.

[6] Chen, G., Firth, M., and Rui, O. M., 2002, "Stock market linkages: evidence from Latin America," *Journal of Banking & Finance*, 26, 1113-1141.

[7] Chiang, M. H., 2001, "The Asymmetric Behavior and Spillover Effects on Stock Index Returns: Evidence on Hong Kong and China," *Pan Pacific Management Review*, 4, 1-21.

[8] Collins, D., and Biekpe, N., 2003, "Contagion: a fear for African equity markets? " *Journal of Economics and Business*, 55, 285-297.

[9] Dornbusch, R., Park, Y. C. and Claessens, S., 2000, "Contagion: Understanding How It Spreads," *The World Bank Research Observer*, 15 (2), 177–197.

[10] Dungey, M., Fry, R., González-Hermosillo, B., and Martin, V., 2006, "Contagion in international bond markets during the Russian and the LTCM crises," *Journal of Financial Stability*, 2, 1-27.

[11] Enders, W. and Granger, C. W., 1998, "Unit-Root Tests and Asymmetric Adjustment with an Example Using the Term Structure of Interest Rates," *Journal of Business and Economic Statistics*, 16, 304-311.

[12] Enders, W. and Siklos, P. L., 2001, "Cointegration and Threshold Adjustment," *Journal of Business and Economic Statistics*, 29, 166-176.

[13] Engle, R. and Granger, C. W., 1987, "Cointegration and Error Correction: Representation, Estimation, and Testing," *Econometrica*, 55, 251-276.

[14] Engle, R. and S. Yoo, 1987, "Forecasting and Testing in Co-integration Systems," *Journal of Econometrics*, 35, 143-159.

[15] Eun, C.S. and Shim, S., 1989, "International Transmission of Stock Market Movements," *Journal of Financial and Quantitative Analysis*, 24, 241-256.

[16] Forbes, K. and Rigobon, R., 2001, "Measuring Contagion : Conceptual and Empirical Issues," *The International Bank for Reconstruction and Development organizing conference of World Bank on "International Financial Contagion: How it Spreads and How it Can Be Stopped"*.

[17] Forbes, K. and Rigobon, R., 2002, "No Contagion, Only Interdependence: Measuring Stock Market Comovements," *Journal of Finance*, 57, 2223-2261.

[18] Ghosh, A., Saidi, R. and Johnson, K.H., 1999, "Who Moves the Asia-Pacific Stock Markets — US or Japan? Empirical Evidence Based on the Theory of Cointegration," *The Financial Review*, 34, 159-170.

[19] Gorton, G. B., 2008, "The Subprime Panic," *NBER Working Paper*, No.w14398, National Bureau of Economic Research.

[20] Hamao, Y., Masulis, R.W. and Ng, V., 1990, "Correlations in Price Changes and Volatility across International Stock Markets," *The Review of Financial Studies*, 3, 281-307.

[21] Johansen, S., 1988, "Statistical Analysis of Cointegration Vectors," *Journal of Economic Dynamics and Control*, 12, 231-254.

[22] Kasa, K., 1992, "Common Stochastic Trends in International Stock Markets," *Journal of Monetary Economics*, 29, 95-124.

[23] Kapetanios, G., Shin, Y., and Snell, A., 2003, "Testing for a unit root in the nonlinear STAR framework," *Journal of Econometrics*, 112, 359-379.

[24] King, M., and Wadhwani, S., 1990, "Transmission of volatility between stock markets," *The Review of Financial Studies*, 3, 5-33.

[25] Koutmos, G., 1998, "Asymmetries in the Conditional Mean and the Conditional Variance: Evidence from Nine Stock Markets," *Journal of Economics and Business*, 50, 277-290.

[26] Lee, S. B. and K. J. Kim, 1993, "Does the October 1987 crash strengthen the co-movements among national stock markets?" *Review of Financial Economics*, 3, 89-102.

[27] Li, W. K. and Lam, K., 1995, "Modelling Asymmetry in Stock Returns by a Threshold Autoregressive Conditional Heteroscedastic Model," *The Statistician*, 44, 333-341.

[28] Liu, Y. A., Pan, M., and Shieh, J., 1998, "International Transmission of Stock Price Movements:Evidence from the U.S. and Five Asian-Pacific Markets," *Journal of Economics and Finance*, 22, 59-69.

[29] Luukkonen, R., Saikkonen, P., and Teräsvirta, T., 1988. "Testing linearity against smooth transition autoregressive models," *Biometrika* 75, 491-499.

[30] Sarantis, N., 2001, "Nonlinearities, Cyclic Behaviour and Predictability in Stock Markets: International Evidence," *International Journal of Forecasting*, 17, 459-482.

[31] Sheng, H. C. and Tu, A. H., 2000, "A Study of Cointegration and Variance Decomposition among Equity Indices before and during the Period of the Asian Financial Crisis," *Journal of Multinational Financial Management*, 10, 345-365.

Chapter 3

Can Monetary Policy Target on Asset Price?
— Evidence from Chinese Real Estate Market[*]

WANG Qing and HAN Xin-tao

School of Finance, Southwestern University of Finance & Economics, China

Abstract

Based on the BEKK model and the GARCH mean-value equation model, this paper analyzes the volatility correlations among real estate price, money supply and economic growth, and examines the impact of various volatilities on economic growth. It has been found out that the volatility of real estate price and the co-volatility between real estate price and money supply have significant impacts on GDP growth rate, and furthermore lead to decline of GDP growth rate. The volatility of real estate price growth rate does not significantly affect economic growth rate volatility, while the co-volatility between money supply and real estate price changes sharply, and the co-volatility between real estate growth rate and economic growth rate does not show significant influence on economic growth rate's volatility. The conclusion is that the volatility of real estate price should be controlled, but currently it is not necessary for the central bank to directly target on real estate price.

With the breakout of sub-prime loan crisis and the bursting of real estate price bubble, global economy goes to severe recession, and the research on relationship between asset price and monetary policy has

[*]This work was supported by Major Program of National Social Science Foundation of China (07&ZD014) and Major Research Program of Philosophy and Social Science of Ministry of Education of China (06JZD0016)

WANG Qing, School of Finance, Southwestern University of Finance &Economics, Professor; research fields: financial economics, capital market

HAN Xin-tao, postgraduate of School of Finance, Southwestern University of Finance & Economics; research fields: financial engineering become a hot issue. More and more central banks are recognizing the influences of asset price on inflation and economic growth.[1] There is no doubt that the real estate price and the bursting of price "bubble" have a far-reaching implication on the monetary policy during the financial crisis.

1. Literature Review

According to the traditional theory, the prices of staple commodities such as real estate can affect the real economy through several known transmission channels. These include consumption effects via the wealth effect (Friedman, 1957), investment effects via Tobin's Q (Tobin, 1969) and the financial accelerator effect. However, there is no consensus on these traditional transmission mechanisms from the theoretical and empirical views. Asset price may play a role on monetary policy transmission. But how important is the role? Whether should asset prices be considered as one of intermediate target of monetary policy? If true, how should they be treated? [2]At present, there are many debates on these issues both from central banks and from the academic world.

---

[1] Recently, an increasing number of central bankers—including some at the Bank of England, Norges Bank, Bank of Canada, and Reserve Bank of New Zealand—have argued that central banks should on rare occasions "lean against" exceptionally large surges in asset prices. A concrete example is provided by the decision of the Swedish central bank in early 2006 to increase its policy rate despite reducing its inflation forecast—a decision justified with an explicit reference to rising household debt and house prices. (World Economic Outlook, April 2008)

[2] There are probably two views on how to deal with asset prices through monetary policy. One view argues that to ensure price and macrostability it is sufficient to focus on the pursuit of low and stable inflation over horizons of one to two years. Given identification and policy calibration difficulties, the best way of addressing potential asset price misalignments is to use monetary policy to cushion the blow of their reversal. This view has been presented by Bernanke and Gertler(1999, 2001), Schwartz(1995, 2002), Borio et al(2002, 2006). The alternative view is that central banks should respond more directly to the perceived asset price misalignment even if inflation is forecast to be on target over the relevant horizon. This view has been presented by Smets(1997), Cecchetti et al (2000), Filardo(2000), Bordo and Jeanne(2002), Detken and Smets (2003).

Borio and Lowe [2002] emphasize that central banks should not focus on inflation alone, because it may miss finding the structure of the financial imbalance, which will put negative effect on banks' and corporations' balance sheets, and further exacerbate financial instability and amplify business cycles. [1] Ahearne [2005] argues that a preemptive response of central bank can diminish the risks that a stronger crash could occur in the real economy later on. Moreover, because restrictive monetary policy has been used to "clean up the mess" after a decline in asset prices, the excessive volatility of asset prices could be avoided. [2] However, Mishkin [2007] doesn't agree to the view that monetary policy "leans against the wind". He argues that policymakers should refrain from targeting on any specific level of asset prices and should respond to changes in asset price only when they affect inflation and output outcomes and expectations because of the difficulties of identifying bubbles in asset price and the uncertainty over the impact of monetary policy on asset prices. [3]

Qian Xiao-an [1998] analyzes the relationship between money supply and asset prices in China's stock market, and finds out that they are less relevant, and the stock index can not be used as a barometer of macro-economy.[4] Qu Qiang [2001] presents his idea from the view of the currency operation, that the current monetary policy should not target on the asset price but pay attention to them, [5] while Yi Gang [2002] finds out that the stock price and the price of goods and services should be considered at the same time when the central bank is formulating monetary policy. [6] Feng Yong-fu [2003] shows that monetary policy intervening in the stock market's volatility is not valid through the establishment of assets- choosing model based on China-specific condition. [7]

Although the scholars, at home and abroad, have done a lot of meaningful research on the relationship between asset price and monetary policy, most empirical studies are only limited in stock market. In a developing country where stock market is not such sound, it is hard to imagine that the adoption of monetary policy to adjust the stock price will succeed. Since the implementation of China's housing reform in 1998, the development of the real estate market is coming into maturity, and the real estate investment has become an important driving force for economic development. There comes also some research involving this area. Wang Wei-an [2005] established a money-market-general-equilibrium model of real estate prices, and studied impacts of endogenous and exogenous money supply on the money market equilibrium. He found out that monetary policy should pay more attention to the real estate prices, but failed to do positive studies on relationship between real estate price and monetary policy in China's context. [8] His conclusions is lack of operational credibility because commodity prices have more or less to do with monetary policy in theory. An investigation report from Shangrao branch of People's Bank of China [2005] studied the transmission mechanism between real estate price and monetary policy by employing the branch data, and drew the conclusion that monetary policy should consider asset price. [9] Because it did not study the relationship between real estate prices' fluctuations and economic growth, the direct intervention of monetary policy in asset price can not simply come to inevitableness.[3] Zhou Jing-kui [2006] studied the fluctuation mechanism of asset price based on interaction between the real estate price and the stock price, but the VAR model in his analysis can only illustrate that one asset price's volatility influences another asset price, and can not capture the joint fluctuation mechanism among different asset prices. [10] Zhang Yue-long [2008] came to conclusion that there is a significant round-leading relationship between China's stock market and real estate market by using Granger causality test, but he ignored the inconsistency of developing process of the real estate market and the stock market, and did not use model to get the co-volatility characteristics of the housing market and the stock market. [11]

At present, the operational vehicle of China's monetary policy is money supply, and the ultimate objective is to maintain stable and rapid economic growth, therefore, it must take two aspects into consideration if asset prices are to be targeted by monetary policy.

---

[3] *"Law of People's Bank of China"* clearly provides that China's objective of monetary policy is to "maintain monetary stability of the currency and promote economic growth", so we believe that asset prices' volatility is bound to affecting economic growth, it is possible that monetary policy will directly target on asset prices.

The first aspect is about the objective of maintaining economy stable growth. It involves the volatility's correlations among three variables. If asset price' s volatility has a large influence on volatility of economic growth and the correlation between asset price volatility and money supply volatility is significant, the central bank can directly control asset price without increasing the total cost. If the asset price volatility is not relevant to the volatility of economic growth while the volatility's correlation between asset price and money supply is significant, the central bank may also directly intervene in asset prices when the asset price and money supply's co-volatility (representing the correlation of two volatilities) has significant impact on the volatility of economic growth, or when the asset price and economic growth's co-volatility significantly affect the volatility in economic growth.

The second aspect is about the objective of maintaining economy rapid growth. It involves the volatility influences of asset price and the money supply on economic growth. If the volatility of asset price has a significant impact on economic growth or the co-volatility of asset price and money supply significantly affects economic growth rate, or the co-volatility of asset price and economic growth affects economic growth rate, asset price should be controlled.

Nowadays, Chinese government pays more attention on quality of economic growth while not on speed of economic growth, so we set up research assumptions of this paper as followings: if asset price volatility has affected the stability of economic growth, and it's possible for monetary policy to intervene in, monetary policy should target on asset price. If asset price volatility has affected the stability of economic growth, but it's not possible for monetary policy to intervene in; or, asset price volatility has only effect on economic growth rate while not on the stability of economic growth, asset price should be controlled, but not necessarily by monetary policy. If asset price volatility has no effect on both the stability of economic growth and economic growth rate, there is no need for central bank to target on asset price.

This paper's contribution mainly lies in three aspects:

Firstly, this paper studies the volatility's relationship among the real estate price, the money supply and the economic growth based on

volatility model, which avoids the limitations of using the VAR model
(cannot directly measure variance) to study asset prices' volatility, and
really unveil time-varying characteristics of volatility (variance) and the
informational transmission mechanism. Furthermore, this model can
measure covariance, which helps to study co-volatilities of different
variables.

Secondly, this paper studies the relationship between asset price and
monetary policy based on China's ultimate objectives of monetary policy
that is to maintain stable and rapid economic growth, which displays
practical significance.

Thirdly, money supply is operational vehicle of monetary policy, so this
paper takes it as the bridge to explore relationships among asset price,
money supply and economic growth.

This paper is arranged as follows: the second part attempts to construct
the MGARCH--BEKK model and GRACH mean-value equation model;
the third part explores the specific relationship of volatilities among real
estate price, money supply and economic growth, as well as impacts of
real estate price volatility and money supply volatility on economic
growth rate; the fourth part draws the conclusion.

2. Construction of Model

2.1 *Volatility Model*

In real economy, there usually have interactions among different markets
or different assets. In order to hedge and avoid risk, and to improve
macroeconomic regulation functions, it is necessary to establish portfolios
among various markets or assets. The multi-GARCH (multivariate
GARCH, MGARCH) model is a good model to measure the volatilities'
correlation relationships. Multi-GARCH model is developed on the basis
of generalized autoregressive conditional heteroskedasticity model
(GARCH model), which has been widely used by taking into account the
time-varying variance of a single-variable time series. But GARCH model
fails to take into account the mutual effects between variance and
covariance. In the existing literature, there are several different types of

multi-GARCH models. One of them is VECH model, but the VECH model has so many parameters that it is difficult to be estimated. Bollerslev, Engle and Wooldridg [1988] developed a bounded VECH model which is known as the diagonal VECH model based on variance-covariance matrixes,[12] but the diagonal VECH model may not portray the full parts of volatility, so it can not measure correlation and spillover effects among many markets. Engle and Kroner [1995] put forward BEKK model on the basis of studies of Baba, Engle, Kraft and Kroner.[13] This model resolved the problem that VECH model must ensure the H matrix is always positive, and allowed conditional variances of many variables to affect each other, which provide basic interpretations for co-volatility among different variables. However, there is still existing "dimension disaster" when a number of variables are involved in the model. Therefore, this paper studies the real estate price and the economic growth's volatility effects through building ternary diagonal BEKK model among money supply (M2), real estate sales price index (Real), gross domestic product (GDP) :

$$\varepsilon_t = H_t^{1/2}\xi_t , \quad \xi_t \sim i.i.dN(O, I)$$

$$H_t = W'W + A'\varepsilon_{t-1}\varepsilon_{t-1}'A + B'H_{t-1}B \qquad (1)$$

Where, W is a lower triangular matrix, A and B are N × N diagonal matrixes. The element a_i of N × N matrix A reflects the ARCH effect of the volatility. The element b_i of N × N matrix B reflects persistence of volatility's transmission, namely the GARCH effect of volatility. The advantages of the model are: 1. the number of parameters is reduced significantly in this model, which is conducive to analyze three or more assets; 2. Variance-covariance matrix is always positive, which guarantees consistency of a specific sequence; 3. The uncertainty of parameters in BEKK model can be solved. Although the spillover effects among market's volatilities can not be considered directly in this model, this model indirectly takes into account other markets' effects while considering volatility's relationship of two markets during solving simultaneous equations. Moreover, the degree of volatility's correlation of two assets can be easily gained in this model. The form of vector matrix for the three-variable-diagonal BEKK (1, 1, 1) model can be written as follows:

$$
\begin{bmatrix} h_{11t} & h_{12t} & h_{13t} \\ h_{21t} & h_{22t} & h_{23t} \\ h_{31t} & h_{32t} & h_{33t} \end{bmatrix} = \begin{bmatrix} w_1 & 0 & 0 \\ w_2 & w_4 & 0 \\ w_3 & w_5 & w_6 \end{bmatrix}^{\mathrm{T}} \begin{bmatrix} w_1 & 0 & 0 \\ w_2 & w_4 & 0 \\ w_3 & w_5 & w_6 \end{bmatrix} + \begin{bmatrix} a_1 & 0 & 0 \\ 0 & a_2 & 0 \\ 0 & 0 & a_3 \end{bmatrix}^{\mathrm{T}} \begin{bmatrix} \varepsilon_{1t\text{-}1}^2 & \varepsilon_{1t\text{-}1}\varepsilon_{2t-1} & \varepsilon_{1t\text{-}1}\varepsilon_{3t-1} \\ \varepsilon_{2t\text{-}1}\varepsilon_{1t-1} & \varepsilon_{2t\text{-}1}^2 & \varepsilon_{2t\text{-}1}\varepsilon_{3t-1} \\ \varepsilon_{3t\text{-}1}\varepsilon_{1t-1} & \varepsilon_{2t\text{-}1}\varepsilon_{1t-1} & \varepsilon_{3t\text{-}1}^2 \end{bmatrix}
$$

$$
\begin{bmatrix} a_1 & 0 & 0 \\ 0 & a_2 & 0 \\ 0 & 0 & a_3 \end{bmatrix} + \begin{bmatrix} b_1 & 0 & 0 \\ 0 & b_2 & 0 \\ 0 & 0 & b_3 \end{bmatrix}^{\mathrm{T}} \begin{bmatrix} h_{11t\text{-}1} & h_{12t\text{-}1} & h_{13t\text{-}1} \\ h_{21t\text{-}1} & h_{22t\text{-}1} & h_{23t\text{-}1} \\ h_{31t\text{-}1} & h_{32t\text{-}1} & h_{33t\text{-}1} \end{bmatrix} \begin{bmatrix} b_1 & 0 & 0 \\ 0 & b_2 & 0 \\ 0 & 0 & b_3 \end{bmatrix} \tag{2}
$$

The separate equations of the conditional variance and the conditional covariance's matrix are:

$$
\begin{aligned}
h_{11t} &= w_1^2 + a_1^2 \varepsilon_{1t-1}^2 + b_1^2 h_{11t-1} \\
h_{12t} &= w_1 w_2 + a_1 a_2 \varepsilon_{1t-1}\varepsilon_{2t-1} + b_1 b_2 h_{12t-1} \\
h_{13t} &= w_1 w_3 + a_1 a_3 \varepsilon_{1t-1}\varepsilon_{3t-1} + b_1 b_3 h_{13t-1} \\
h_{22t} &= w_2^2 + w_4^2 + a_2^2 \varepsilon_{2t-1}^2 + b_2^2 h_{22t-1} \\
h_{23t} &= w_2 w_3 + w_4 w_5 + a_2 a_3 \varepsilon_{2t-1}\varepsilon_{3t-1} + b_2 b_3 h_{23t-1} \\
h_{33t} &= w_3^2 + w_5^2 + w_6^2 + a_3^2 \varepsilon_{3t-1}^2 + b_3^2 h_{33t-1}
\end{aligned} \tag{3}
$$

Where, h_{iit} represents conditional variance of certain variable, h_{ijt} represents conditional covariance between two variables, $a_i a_j$ reflects ARCH effect impact on future co-volatility, $b_i b_j$ reflects volatility persistence effect on future co-volatility. i,j=1,2,3. 1 stands for money supply growth rate, 2 stands for real estate sales price index growth rate, and 3 stands for economic growth rate.

If the volatility spillover effects don't exist among money supply, real estate sales price index and GDP, parameters $a_1 a_2$、 $a_1 a_3$、 $a_2 a_3$、 $b_1 b_2$、 $b_1 b_3$ and $b_2 b_3$ are not significantly different from zero in statistics.

The parameters of above diagonal BEKK model can be estimated through maximizing the following log-likelihood function on the condition of normal assumption.

$$l(\theta) = -\frac{TN}{2}\log 2\pi - \frac{1}{2}\sum_{t=1}^{T}(\log|H_t| + \varepsilon_t' H_t^{-1}\varepsilon_t) \qquad (4)$$

Where, θ represents unknown parameters to be estimated, N is the number of assets, T is the number of observations, and other symbols have the same meaning as previous model. The maximum likelihood estimation for θ is progressive, hence, the traditional process of statistical inference can be used.

2.2 Growth Model

In order to study the effects on economic growth rate caused by real estate price volatility and the co-volatility between real estate price and money supply, the mean-value equation of GARCH model where GDP changes over time is established.

$$y_{3t} = \alpha + \sum_{1}^{i}\beta_i y_{3t-i} + \sum_{1}^{i}\gamma_i u_{3t-i} + u_{3t} \qquad (5)$$

Where, y_{3t} represents GDP growth, u_{1t} represents residuals, α represents constant, β_i and γ_i are parameters.

The conditional variance and the conditional covariance from (2) and (3) are added into the mean-value equation to observe whether factors are significant or not. The model is as follows:

$$y_{3t} = \alpha + \sum_{1}^{i}\beta_i y_{3t-i} + \sum_{1}^{i}\gamma_i u_{3t-i} + \delta h_{22} + \xi h_{12} + \phi h_{13} + \varphi h_{23} + \eta h_{11} + u_{3t} \qquad (6)$$

If factor δ is significant, it suggests that the volatility of real estate price has a great impact on economic growth. If factor ξ is significant, it suggests that the co-volatility between real estate price and money supply has a great impact on economic growth. If factor ϕ is significant, it suggests that the co-volatility between real estate price and economic growth has a great effect on economic growth. If factor η is significant, it suggests that the volatility of money supply has a great effect on economic growth.

3. Empirical Research

3.1 *Data Collection and Adjustment*

In order to assure data adequate and reasonable, the paper takes the money supply, the housing sales price index and the GDP's quarterly data from the first quarter of 1998 (when the implementation of China's housing reform) to the second quarter of 2008 as samples. Observations of each variable are 42. Since money supply is monthly data, we use arithmetic average method to compute the quarterly data. The housing sales price index is used as representative of the real estate sales price. At the same time, in order to eliminate heteroscedasticity, we add 100 to the data value and take their logarithm forms. $m2_{1t}$ represents the money supply index at t quarter, and the money supply growth rate is expressed as: $y_{1t} = \log m2_{1t} - \log m2_{1t-1}$; $\mathrm{Re}\,al_{2t}$ represents the real estate sales price index at t quarter, and the growth rate of real estate sales price index is expressed as: $y_{2t} = \log \mathrm{Re}\,al_{2t} - \log \mathrm{Re}\,al_{2t-1}$. gdp_{3t} represents GDP at t quarter, and the growth rate of GDP is expressed as: $y_{3t} = \log gdp_{3t} - \log gdp_{3t-1}$. All data of this paper are from CEI statistical database.

3.2 *Basic Characteristics of Statistics*

Money supply (M2) growth rate, real estate price index (Real) and GDP growth rate are analyzed. Table 1 shows the results of descriptive statistics from the first quarter of 1998 to the second quarter of 2008. Figure 1 shows variables changing trends. The Real growth rate has the biggest gap between the maximum value and the minimum value (11.4%), the largest standard deviation (3.29%) and the biggest variation coefficient (0.73), which shows the real estate price's volatility is the greatest among three. GDP growth rate has the smallest volatility in the past decade, which confirms the rapid and stable growth of China's economy. At the same time, the average increase rate of money supply (M2) is higher than that of GDP by about 6.4% that is higher than average inflation rate 1.6% in this decade, which shows a relative loosening monetary policy during this period[4].

---

[4] Data source: China statistics yearbook 2008.

Table 1. Results of Descriptive Statistics

variable	max	min	mean	median	S.T.	Var. Coef.
M2growth rate (%)	12.33	21.00	16.17	16.47	2.27	0.14
Real growth rate (%)	-0.40	11.00	4.63	4.55	3.39	0.73
GDP growth rate (%)	7.20	12.20	9.70	9.85	1.46	0.15

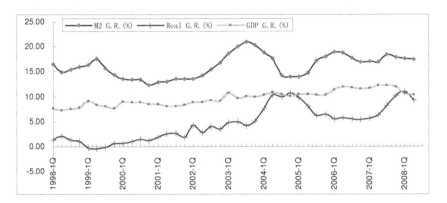

Figure 1. The changing trends of the Money supply (M2) growth rate, the growth rate of real estate price index (Real) and the GDP growth rate

Figure 1 shows steady GDP moving trend, which is also in line with the government's economical goal that maintains "steady and relatively fast growth". Money supply and real estate price shows relative large volatilities, particularly real estate price lagging money supply for about one year. In the mean time, the real estate growth rate is almost smaller than GDP growth rate. So, although China's real estate growth rate displays dramatic changes, it seems still under the control of economic changes.

Three series are found steady at the 5% confidence level in unit root test.

3.3 Empirical Analysis based on MGARCH-BEKK Model

Table 2 shows the results of the estimated parameters. Only b1 and b3 are significant at 95% confidence level. b_1b_3 (0.75×1.01= 0.7575) shows that the co-volatility between money supply and economic growth has the strongest GARCH effect, which implies co-volatility of money supply and economic growth is persistent, and the current relationship between money supply and economic growth will affect their future relationship. In other word, it suggests that there inevitably exists a volatility spillover effect between money supply and economic growth. Factor a1, a2 and a3 are not significant, which shows that the co-volatilities among real estate price, money supply and economic growth do not have obvious ARCH effect, current real estate price, money supply and economic growth having no strong impact on their future values. But it can not rule out the possibility that their interactions have ARCH effect. Through BDS test [5](See Table 3), we find out that only the co-volatility between money supply and economic growth have ARCH effect. To sum up, the real estate growth rate doesn't have significant volatility spillover effect on economic growth rate.

Table 2. Results of MGARCH-BEKK Model Estimation

Parameter	a_1	a_2	a_3	b_1	b_2	b_3
Value of estimation	0.53	0.76	0.10	0.75	0.45	1.01
T statistics	1.52	1.30	0.17	2.17	0.66	13.37
P value	0.13	0.19	0.87	0.03	0.51	0.00

Table 3. Results of the BDS Test for Money Supply, Housing Sales Price Index and GDP

Conditional variance	BDS statistics(two dimensions)	Z statistics	P value
h_{12}	0.034489	1.70248	0.0887
h_{13}	0.079454	5.95878	0.0000
h_{23}	-0.008836	-0.56216	0.5740

---

[5] This statistics is developed by Brook、Dechert and Scheinkman(1987),zero assumption is no ARCH effect.

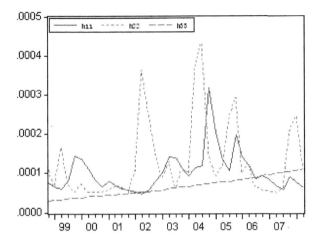

Figure 2. The changing trend of Conditional variance

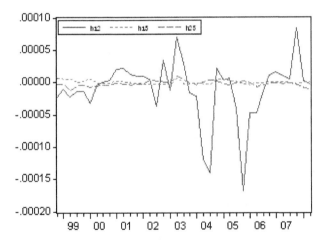

Figure 3. The changing trend of conditional covariance

Figure 2 and figure 3 shows the changing trends of variance and covariance of money supply, real estate price and economic growth respectively. As shown from figure 2, the volatility of economic growth rate presents slow and steady increase during the decade, but the volatilities of money supply and real estate price change sharply. It is also found out that the volatilities of money supply and house price growth rate move closely, and the volatility of money supply growth rate lags behind the volatility of house price growth rate about 1 to 4 quarters, and the volatility degree of money supply is smaller than that of house price .

Since the real estate price shows a close and lagging response to growth rate of money supply, this seems to mean that the central bank's monetary policy has always targeted on the real estate price' s volatility, or the monetary policy has naturally smoothed the volatility of housing price. If the latter is true, it reveals that the volatility of money supply is significantly related to housing prices, and the central bank need not to intervene in asset prices. But the key point is, whether there is possibility for central bank to intervene in real estate price? We further exam the correlation relationships of volatilities. Figure 3 shows that the co-volatility between money supply growth rate and economic growth rate, as well as the co-volatility between housing price growth rate and economic growth rate almost keep unchanged in the vicinity of zero, but the co-volatility between money supply growth rate and housing price growth rate changes sharply. This puts forth a challenge for monetary policy's direct intervention in asset prices, because the instability of co-volatility between the money supply growth rate and the house price growth rate makes it hard for monetary policy to operate. Moreover, as seen from figures 2 and 3, the co-volatility between housing price growth rate and economic growth rate, and that between money supply growth rate and housing price growth rate are much smaller than the single volatility themselves. This reveals that the co-volatility between housing prices growth rate and economic growth rate, and that between money supply growth rate and housing price growth rate do not have significant impact on economic growth.

There are some theories explaining the mechanism that money supply affects real economy through real estate price, such as Tobin q theory (Tobin, 1969), permanent revenue theory (Friedman, 1957), and life-cycle theory (Modigliani, 1963). During which, the change of real estate price reflects complicated money demand. Wang Wei-an (2005) pointed out that the impact of real estate price changing money demand is reflected in three aspects: 1. wealth effect; 2. transaction effect; 3. substitution effect. Wealth effect and transaction effect increase the demand for money, but substitution effect reduces the demand for money. As the result, the effects of the real estate prices' volatility on the money demand are uncertain. It is just because that these opposite effects of the real estate prices showing no significant roles to the economic growth and these insignificant relationships have a long-term persistency, the central bank doesn't have to directly regulate real estate prices' volatility in practice.

In practice, in recent years the central bank has implemented special regulations on real estate market for three times. The first regulation occurred in 2003, in order to cool down overheat of real estate investment, and to stop illegal lending and deterioration of macro-indicators such as house price-to-income, real estate investment to fixed asset investment, personal home loans' growth rate to personal income growth rate, the central bank strengthened the management of real estate credit business through issuing the No 121st document *"To further tighten real estate credit"* on June 13th. Although the document clearly showed that the central bank was worrying about the price risk concealed in overheated real estate investment, China's real estate prices did not stop pacing up from early 2002 to late 2004 with the accumulated increase rate of 25%[6]. The central bank's intervention in the real estate market didn't play any part at all.

The second regulation occurred during 2005 and 2006. In March 2005, the central bank adjusted the individual home loan policy of commercial Banks. The People's Bank of China and other relevant ministries promulgated the *"National 8 rules"* and *"National 6 rules"* to further tighten the real estate loans and avoid risk of loans in April 2005 and in May of the following year. The People's Bank of China implemented a series of financial regulation and controlling policies in 2006. It raised the benchmark lending rate by 0.27 percent for twice and raised deposit reserve rate by 0.5 percent for three times. It released *"Views on adjusting housing supplies' structure to stabilize prices"* on May 29th of the same year, which banned banks to lending to the real estate enterprises whose capital ratios were less than 35%. to some extent, A series of monetary policies and other ministries' measures controlled the real estate prices'

---

[6] Data resource: China Statistics Yearbook 2008.

volatility (the real estate price increase rate remained 5.5 percent or so during this period[7]), and at the same time, the macro-economic growth rate reached 10.7 percent in 2006 without being affected. This implies that even if the central bank's monetary policy can target on real estate prices, there is still a lot of uncertainties to work on real economy.

The third regulation was implemented for the simultaneous sharp rise of the real estate market and the stock market in 2007. The central bank and the CBRC issued "Notice on strengthening commercial real estate credit management " in September. This rule strictly separated the housing consumption and housing investment. It still encouraged people to purchase the first owner-occupied house and didn't adjust down payment ratio, but the down payment ratio was raised to 40% for the second house. In December of the same year, the central bank and the CBRC published *"Supplementary notice on strengthening commercial real estate credit management"*, which implemented strict measures for the second as well as over two houses. This year, the central bank raised deposit reserve rate for ten times, which should impose substantial impact on real estate prices. As a result, the growth rate of real estate prices still increased nearly 6 percent within a year[8], and the economic growth rate began to decline from 2008. This implies that the central bank's monetary policy didn't attain effectiveness in terms of regulating and controlling real estate prices, but resulted in lower economic growth to some extent.

Therefore, through the analysis in theory and practice, in order to "realize rapid economic growth under the prerequisite of guaranteeing stable economic growth", it is not necessary that the central bank uses monetary policy to regulate asset prices.

4. Empirical Analysis based on GARCH Mean-Value-Equation Model

A reasonable means-value equation is established according to SC and AIC criteria:

---

[7] Data resource: China Statistics Yearbook 2008.
[8] Data resource: China Statistics Yearbook 2008.

$$y_{3t} = \alpha + \beta y_{3t-1} + \gamma u_{3t-1} + u_{3t} \qquad (7)$$

Then, we put conditional variance and conditional covariance of BEKK model into mean-value-equation model.

$$y_{3t} = \alpha + \beta y_{3t-1} + \gamma u_{3t-1} + \delta h_{22} + \xi h_{12} + \phi h_{13} + \varphi h_{23} + \eta h_{11} + u_{3t} \qquad (8)$$

The estimated results of all parameters at the 5% confidence level are presented in Table 4:

Table 4. Results of Mean-Value-Equation Model

Parameter	δ	ξ	ϕ	φ	η
Value of estimation	-2814.84	-5477.11	-24897.38	30130.99	-724.04
T statistics	-2.25	-2.16	-0.77	1.20	-0.34
P value	0.03	0.04	0.45	0.24	0.74

As we have seen, only δ and ξ are significant at the 5% confidence level, which means there are only the volatility of real estate price and the co-volatility between real estate price and money supply having significant impact on GDP growth rate. Moreover, the volatilities lead to decline on GDP growth rate. Therefore, from the point of view of maintaining rapid economic growth, the real estate price has to be controlled.

5. Conclusions

This paper studies the dynamic changes in the relationship among real estate price, money supply and economic growth based on the diagonal BEKK model and the GARCH mean-value-equation model.

Firstly, as far as the volatility correlation is concerned, only money supply and GDP have significant characteristics of time-varying variance and persistent volatility. The volatility spillover effect between real estate price growth rate and economic growth rate is not obvious. The co-volatility between money supply and real estate price changes sharply, and the co-volatility between real estate price growth rate and money supply growth rate does not show great influence on economic growth rate's volatility, which interprets that it's not possible and necessary for central bank to target on the real estate price.

Secondly, as far as the growth rate is concerned, the volatility of real estate price and the co-volatility between real estate price and money supply have significant impacts on GDP growth rate, furthermore, their volatilities will lead to decline in GDP growth rate, so the volatility of real estate price should be controlled.

In general, in order to reach the ultimate objective of monetary policy, that is, "to realize rapid economic growth under the prerequisite of guaranteeing stable economic growth", it is not necessary that the central bank uses monetary policy to regulate asset prices. The real estate price can be controlled through various means such as fiscal policy, land policy, some administrative measures, and even welfare policy[9].

References

[1] Borio C and Lowe P., 2002, "Assessing the risk of banking crises", BIS Quarterly Review, December.
[2] Ahearne, Alan G., JohnAmmer, Brian M. Doyle, Linda S. Kole, and Robert F. Martin, 2005, "House Prices and Monetary Policy: A Cross-Country Study", FRB International Finance Discussion Paper, No.841.
[3] Mishkin, Frederic S., 2007, "Housing and the Monetary Transmission Mechanism", paper presented at the Federal Reserve Bank of Kansas City 31st Economic Policy Symposium, August 31–September 1.
[4] Qian X A. 1998, "Impact of Changes in Asset Prices on Monetary Policy", *Economic Research Journal*, 1: 70-76.
[5] Qu Q. 2001, "Asset Prices and Monetary Policy", *Economic Research Journal*, 7:60-67.
[6] Yi G, Wang Z. 2002, "Monetary Policy and Financial Assets Price", *Economic Research Journal*, 2: 13-20.

[9] As early as April 10, 2005, Wu XL, the deputy Governor of the PBC, made a speech entitled "The impetus and impacts of China's monetary policy and financial policies on the real estate" at the real estate finance forum sponsored by Policy Research Office of the CPC Central Committee . She stressed that in addition to the central bank's monetary policy, China need joint efforts including land policy, tax policy, credit and financial policies in regulating real estate price' s excessive growth.

[7]   Feng Y F. 2003, "Can Monetary Policy Interfere with the Excessive Fluctuation of Stock Price?", *Economic Research Journal*, 1: 38-44.

[8]   Wang W A, He C. 2005, "Real Estate Prices and Monetary Supply and Demand: Empirical Events and Theory Hypothesis", *The Study of Finance and Economics*, 5: 17-28.

[9]   Research Group of Shangrao City Branch of the PBC, 2005, "The Study of Asset Price Bubble and Optimal Monetary Policy: A Case Study of Real Estate Market", *Journal of Financial Research*, 11: 144-155.

[10]   [Zhou J k. 2006, "The Research on Volatility Mechanisms of China's asset price: 1998~2005 ---based on the interaction between the Real Estate Prices and Stock Prices", Shanghai Economic Review, 4:21-29.

[11]   Zhang Y L, Wu J. 2006, "The Research on Stage Relationship between China's Real Estate Market and Stock Market's Volatility", *China Real Estate*, 1:29-30.

[12]   Bollerslev T,Engle R F, Wooldridg J.,1988,"A capital asset pricing model with time varing covariances", Jorunal of Political Economy, 96:116-131.

[13]   Engle R F, Kroner K F., 1995, "Mulitivariate stimultaneous generalized ARCH ", Econometric Theory, 11:122-150.

Chapter 4

Relationship Banking and Firm Profitability[*]

Shigeru Uchida

Professor, Faculty of Economics Nagasaki University, Japan

Sarwar U. Ahmed

Associate Professor, School of Business, Independent University, Bangladesh

Abstract

Small and medium enterprises (SMEs) having less creditworthiness and reputation compared to bigger firms are in greater need of establishing long-term relationship with banks to ensure continued supply of funds. Accordingly, this study aims at summarizing the findings of the empirical analysis regarding the impact of relationship banking on the performance of SMEs of Japan. The findings of the analysis indicated that, having multiple banking relationships implies rather weak profitability status of a corporate firm. Although relationship banking leading towards corporate shareholding raises profitability of the SMEs, increased supply of credit conversely reduces the profits. But overall, relationship banking has positive impact on the profitability of SMEs while there are other reasons to explain the negative relationship between credit and profitability.

1. Introduction

Relationship banking can be defined as a long-term relationship between the financial intermediary and the corporate firm developed by repeated interactions transpired from diversified transactions, accumulation of

---

[*]S. Uchida is grateful for partial support from Japan Society for the Promotion of Science (Grant-in-Aids for Scientific Research (C), 18530237).

specific information and major loan concentration (Uchida and Ahmed, 2008). It plays an important role on the performance of the corporate firms, particularly small and medium enterprises (SMEs). Big firms with good reputation and creditworthiness, establishing relationship with particular bank or banks does not count much as they can raise funds comparatively easily. But for SMEs relationship banking becomes vital. Unless their credit worthiness is known to the lender for a considerable period of time, it would be very difficult for them to get credit on a speedy basis and rescued during financial distress. A long-term relationship allows the lending bank to gather adequate information regarding the future prospect and credit worthiness of the borrowing firm and to decide whether to extend credit, how to price it and the extent of collateral. Thus it would be interesting to investigate whether relationship banking actually contributes in the profitability performance of the SMEs.

Table 1. Possible impact of relationship banking

Main features of relationship banking	Overall Evaluation
Increased credit availability	O
Lower investment sensitivity to liquidity	O/Δ
Less risk of client firms	O/Δ
Risk sharing through interest rates	Δ/O
Effective handling of financial distress; timely management intervention	O/Δ
Firms faring worse in economy-wide financial turbulence (when banks themselves are in distress)	Δ/O
Monopoly rents charged on client firms	Δ
Faster corporate growth	X/Δ
Higher corporate efficiency and profits	X/Δ

Note: O Yes; O/ Δ largely yes; Δ /O weakly yes; Δ Mixed, X/ Δ Largely no
Source: S. Nam (2004)

There are various theoretical and empirical studies explaining the impact of relationship banking on availability of credit, rescuing in financial distress, reducing risk and improving the performance of the borrowing firms (for example, Fukuda and Hirota (1996); Mori (1994);

Nam (2004); Hoshi et al. (1990); Okazaki and Horiuchi (1992)). The findings of these studies are rather diverse. Some found positive impact in some of the above factors and some did not. S. Nam (2004) summarized a literature review of the empirical evidence on relationship banking features as shown in **Table 1**. According to this table, relationship banking did not contribute in raising corporate efficiency and profits. But the Small and Medium Size Enterprise Agency (2000) concluded that SMEs with close relationship with banks (with bank shareholding in the firm) tend to have higher profits (ROA), sales growth, presences in new business and so on. Based on these contrasting results of the role of relationship banking on the profitability of SMEs, this paper aims to investigate this role by conducting an empirical study on the exchange listed SMEs in Japan.

2. Relationship Banking in Japan

2.1 *Nature of Relationship Banking in Japan*

The most typical and conventional nature of relationship banking can be found in Japan, where the size of the banking sector to GNP is the largest. This typical kind of relationship is also popularly known as *main-bank relationship; the relationship between a client company and its main-bank.*

In Japan there are five main aspects of relationship banking, such as: bond issue related; bank loans; shareholding; payment settlement account; services; and supply of management and information resources (Aoki et al. (1995)). As shown in the **Fig. 1**, financing aspect can refer to bond issue related services and bank loans, of which bank loan has traditionally been the key one. While the monitoring and governance aspects of the relationship are settlement accounts, stockholding and supply of management resources. In Japan this second dimension of the bank-firm relationship is ensured by the following activities:

2.1.1 *Stockholding of Firms*

The main banks in Japan hold a significant portion of the firm's share and usually are in the top five shareholders of the client firm.

2.1.2 Supply of Management Resources

Under Japanese banking system, bank often sends its mangers as directors or auditors on the board of client firms (Aoki et al. (1995), Kigyo Keiretsu Soran, 1992).

Fig. 1. Aspects of relationship banking

2.1.3 Loan Syndication

The main bank in Japan has also been expected to play the leading role in case of corporate distress, to organize financial rescue, restructuring and to bear a disproportionate share of the costs of financial assistance through interest exemptions or deferrals, loan rescheduling, loan losses and new fund supply relative to the syndicate as a whole (Aoki et al. (1995)).

2.2 Effect of Relationship Banking in Japan

The effect of relationship banking practices in Japan as evident in various theoretical and literature studies can be summarized as follows:

2.2.1 *Credit Availability*

Numerous studies concluded that Japanese firms with relationship bank enjoy easier access to credit and did not face liquidity crisis (Fukuda and Hirota (1996); Mori (1994)). Also there are studies drawing opposite conclusions too. For example, Hayashi (2000) finds no evidence that relationship banking esteemed from main banking did help the firm in meeting liquidity crisis.

2.2.2 *Rescuing in Financial Distress*

Japanese firms with strong main bank relationship seem to have been better protected in times of financial distress than those without such relationship (Nam (2004); Hoshi, Kashyap, and Scharfstein (1990); Okazaki and Horiuchi (1992)).

2.2.3 *Reduction of Risk*

Relationship banking had contributed in reducing risk of corporate borrowers by assisting the firms in times of financial distress and reducing corporate fluctuations (Uchida (1997); Kawai, Hashimoto and Izumida (1996)).

As to reducing risk, it has been well known by the economic analysis of information that both main bank and company could have the effect of risk sharing by minimizing the level of asymmetry of information in between business and management (Uchida(1995)).

2.2.4 *Performance of Borrowing Firms*

Relationship banking does not indicate that this improves the performance of the corporate firms. Charging of higher interest rates was evident by main banks (Hosono (1997); Weinstein and Yafeh (1998)).

Bargaining power and monopolistic level in loan negotiations between main bank and client firm could also become key factor to influence the corporate performance.

3. Methodology

3.1 *Data*

Exchange listed SMEs in Japan have been selected as a source of data by following the criteria set in the *Small and Medium Enterprises Basic Law 1999*, where the term "small and medium enterprise" (SME) refers in general to enterprises with capital of not in excess of 300 million yen or number of employees, 300 or fewer employees, Wholesale industries; 100 million yen or less, 100 or fewer, and Retail industries and service industries; 50 million yen or less, 100 or fewer, respectively. By following this definition we have picked up the three yearly time series balance sheet data (March 2005-March 2007) of 114 SMEs from *Kaisha Shikiho, 2007* and conducted the analysis. During the final analysis the numbers of SMEs are again reduced due to non-availability of complete data regarding all the required factors.

3.2 *Models*

A hypothetical multivariate model is developed to test the relationship between the return on assets (ROA) of SMEs with some other relevant factors. The best subset approach of model selection is used for identifying the most influencing variable (Levine *et al.* (2002)). The steps followed in the model selection under this approach are outlined in **Fig. 2**. Accordingly, two criteria are used to choose among models with different combination of independent variables. The first criterion is variance inflationary factor (VIF), used for measuring collinearity among the explanatory variables. VIF_j, the variance inflationary factor for variable j is defined in Equation 1.

$$VIF_j = \frac{1}{1 - r_j^2} \tag{1}$$

Where, r_j^2 is the coefficient of multiple determination of explanatory variable X_j with all other X variables. As a rule of thumb all VIF should be less than 5.0 to prove that there is no collinearity among the explanatory variables (Snee (1973)).

A second criterion used for evaluating competing models is C_p statistic, developed by Mallows and is defined as shown in Equation 2 (Neter *et al.* (1996)).

$$C_p = \frac{(1 - r_k^2)(n - T)}{1 - r_T^2} - (n - 2(k + 1)) \qquad (2)$$

Where,

K = number of independent variables included in a regression model

T = total number of parameters (including the intercept) to be estimated in the full regression model.

r_k^2 = coefficient of multiple determination for a regression model that has k independent variables

r_T^2 = coefficient of multiple determination for a full regression model that contains all T estimated parameters

As a selection standard the goal is to find models whose Cp is close to or below (k+1). Statistical software PH stat2 is used for the statistical analysis.

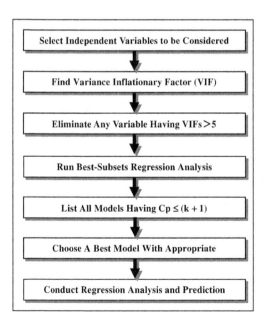

Fig. 2. Procedure in model building by best-subsets approach

4. Empirical Analysis

4.1 *The Hypothetical Model*

In order to identify the factors, which influences the performance of the corporate firms (Profitability) we have constructed a hypothetical model. The objective is to see how relationship banking is affecting the performance of the corporate firms. As a parameter to represent profitability we have selected time series mean of return on assets (ROA) of the companies. The factors, which are hypothesized to have influence on a firm's profitability, can be summarized by the following conceptual model:

$$\text{Profitability (ROA)} = f(\text{SAL, AGE, EMP, DER, SHA, NBK, dREL}) \qquad (3)$$

The model consists of variables that are hypothetically assumed to have an influence on profitability of a corporate firm, such as: sales volume, debt-equity ratio, percentage of holding share by banks and number of banks. Accordingly, firm size is measured by the log of sales to test the impact of power and efficiency on profitability of the firms (PRF). Next, debt-equity ratio (DER) is included to test the impact of financial leverage. Firm age is included to get the effect of length of operation, as more profitable firms are more likely to survive in the long run. Percentage of holding share by banks (SHA) and number of banks (NBK) are involved to check how the share and presence of banking institutions affect the profitability of the firms. Finally, to investigate whether multilateral financing is less profitable than bilateral financing, a dummy (dREL) is included.

The explanation of the variables and the descriptive statistics are presented in **Table 2**, containing their expected relationship sign with the dependent variable return on assets (ROA). The debt-equity ratio in the table is calculated as follows:

$$Debt - equity Ratio (DER) = \frac{Total Fixed Liabilities}{Total Share Holders' Equity} \qquad (4)$$

Where, fixed liabilities include loan from banks. A higher debt-equity ratio implies the dominance of bank loans as a source of financing.

Table 2. Variables and descriptive statistics (n =113)

Variable Name	Description	Mean	Standard Deviation	Expected Sign in Regression Model
ROA	The dependent variable is the time series mean of return on assets	5.77	4.7	
SAL	Log of time series mean of the total sales volume of the company in million yen	8.19	1.10	+
AGE	The age of the firm relative to their founding date	27	23	+
EMP	Time series mean of number of employees	159	343	+
DER	Debt-equity ratio of the company †	3.11	1.26	?
SHA	Percentage of share held by financial institutions	1.33	2.50	?
NBK	Number of banks the company maintains transacting relationship	3.60	1.81	-
dREL	The multiple bank relationship dummy. 1 when the firm maintains multiple relationship, 0 otherwise.	0.89	0.31	-

†See equation 4 for the formula

Table 3. Selected models by best subsets analysis for reducing the number of explanatory variables

Model No.	Variables in the Model	Cp	k	R Square	Adj. R Square	Std. Error
1	AGE, NBK,	0.90	3	0.62	0.54	9.28
2	AGE, EMP, NBK,	2.05	4	0.62	0.53	9.30
3	AGE, EMP, NBK, dREL	3.28	5	0.64	0.55	9.30
4	AGE, DER, NBK	2.26	4	0.62	0.53	9.30

Table 4. Results of the regression analysis by using best subsets approach to model building(Dependent Variable = ROA)

Variables	Coefficient (t-stat) [n=113]
Constant	15.38 (2.18)
AGE	-0.11(-2.45) *
EMP	0.002(1.07) *
NBK	-0.79 (-1.39)*
dREL	-3.05 (-0.91) *

Note: * Indicates that the coefficient is statistically significant at least at 0.10 level.

4.2 *Selected Model and Results*

Best subset analysis is applied by including the variables mentioned in equation 3. The results are summarized in **Tables 3-4**. As shown in **Table 3**, due to the subset analysis, out of 137 models we have found 4 models having C_p statistic<(k+1) and almost similar adjusted R Square and standard error. For lack of space only the best models are shown here. Finally, on the basis of the significance of the regression coefficients (P value) and lowest C_p statistic, model 3 is selected as the best model.

Thus from the selected model we have found that only AGE, EMP, NBK and dREL variables are worth of retaining in the model and are statistically significant. Where AGE, NBK and dREL are negatively related, on the other hand EMP is positively related with the dependent variable ROA (see **Table 4**).

4.3 *Test of Collinearity*

Collinearity refers to situations where some of the explanatory variables are highly correlated with each other (Levine *et al.* (2002)). This causes extreme fluctuations in the regression coefficients depending on the inclusion of the various independent variables. In order to check for collinearity, we have calculated variance inflationary factor (VIF) for each explanatory variables. **Table 5** summarizes the VIF for the independent variables with all other explanatory variables. Snee (1973), observed that VIF less than 5.0 indicates absence of collinearity among the explanatory variables. Thus, from the table we can see that, all the explanatory variables have VIF< 1.5, thus no fear of collinearity exists.

Table 5. Test of Collinearity through VIF

Variables	VIF
SAL and all other explanatory variables	1.26
AGE and all other explanatory variables	1.40
DER and all other explanatory variables	1.16
SHA and all other explanatory variables	1.23
NBK and all other explanatory variables	1.38
EMP and all other explanatory variables	1.15

5. Concluding Remarks

In this study we have taken a modest attempt to empirically examine the impact of relationship banking on the performance of the Japanese corporate firms, particularly the exchange listed small and medium sized enterprises. The findings of the study can be summed up as follows:

1) Negative relationship of number of banks firms maintaining relationship with profitability (ROA) denotes that, relationship banking does count in improving the profitability performance of the firms.

2) The negative coefficient of dREL indicates that, maintaining multiple relationship decreases ROA by 3.05 percent. Hence, relationship banking is important in explaining firm profitability.

3) On the other hand, the negative relationship between AGE with profitability (ROA) indicates that older firms would have difficulty in survival having lower profitability. Whereas, positive relation of number of employees with profitability reflects more profitable firms are able to accommodate more employees.

Table 6. Impact of relationship banking on profitability of SMEs

	Impact on Profitability	Evaluation Mark
Multiple banking	−	○
Maximizing shareholders wealth	+	○
Higher corporate efficiency and profits	+	○

Note: O = Yes, Δ= Moderate, X = No and ? = Not confirmed

The varied impact of relationship banking on profitability of SMEs can be expressed through **Table 6**. Negative impact of multiple banking suggests that relationship banking does count on the performance of the SME's in Japan. Therefore, the form of banking arrangement is important in explaining the efficiency and profitability of firms.

Small and new firms with high growth potential stick with single bank because of convenience. When growth slows down, they need to look for other banks to meet their financial needs.

However, this study is based on data of short time period. More detailed studies and inclusion of more time series data are needed to establish and support these findings. These areas leave the scope for further studies.

Acknowledgements

This study is supported by the study grant of the Japan Society for the Promotion of Science(JSPS).

References

[1]   Aoki, M. and Patrick, H. (1995), The Japanese Main Bank System: its Relevance for Developing and Transforming Economies, *Oxford Univ. Press.*
[2]   Fukuda, A. and S. Hirota (1996) Main bank relationships and capital structure in Japan, *Journal of Japanese and International Economics*, 10, pp.250-261.
[3]   Hayashi, F. (2000) The main bank system and corporate investment: an empirical assessment, in M. Aoki and G. R. Saxonhouse, eds., Finance, Governance and Competitiveness in Japan, *Oxford: Oxford University Press.*

[4]   Hoshi, T., A. Kashyap and D. Scharfstein (1990) The role of bank in reducing the costs of financial distress in Japan, *Journal of Financial Economics*, 27, pp.67-88.

[5]   Hosono, K. (1997) R&D Expenditure and the choice between private and public debt- do the Japanese main banks extract the frim's rents? *Institute of Economic Research*, Hitotsubashi University, Discussion Paper No. 353.

[6]   Kawai, M., Hashimoto, J. and Izumida, S. (1996) Japanese firma in financial distress and main banks: analysis of interest-rate premia, *Japan and the World Economy*, 8, pp.175-194.

[7]   Levine, D. M., D. Stephan, T. C. Krehbiel and M. L. Berenson (2002) *Statistics for managers using microsoft excel*. Third edition, Prentice Hall, New Jersey.

[8]   Mori, A. (1994) Investment of corporations and the role of main banks: empirical studies based on the information theories, *Financial Review*, 33, Policy research Institute, Ministry of Finance.

[9]   Nam, S (2004) Relationship banking and its role in corporate governance, *Research Paper Series*, 56, ADB Institute.

[10]   Neter, J., M. Kutner, C. Nachtsheim and W. Wasserman (1996) *Applied linear statistical models*. Fourth edition, Irwin, Homewood, IL.

[11]   Okazaki, T. and A. Horiuchi (1992) Investment and the main bank. (Horiuchi, A. and N. Yoshino Eds.), *Structural Analysis of the Japanese Financial System* (in Japanese), University of Tokyo Press.

[12]   Small and Medium Size Enterprise Agency (2000) White paper on small and medium enterprises for FY1999, Towards the age of management innovation and new business creation. p.595.

[13]   Snee, R. D. (1973) Some aspects of non-orthogonal data analysis, Part I. Developing prediction equations, *Journal of Quality Technology*, No.5, pp.67-79.

[14]   Toyo Keizai Inc. (2007) *Kaisha Shikiho* (in Japanese), Toyo Keizai Inc.

[15]   Uchida, K. (1997) Main bank relations and evaluation of corporation: mainly about the risk evaluation in the stock market, *Japan Financial Review 22* (in Japanese).

[16]   Uchida, S. (1995) *Deregulation and Bank Competition*, (in Japanese), Chikura Shoboh Inc.

[17]   Uchida, S. and Ahmed, S. U ,"The Role of Relationship Banking on the Performance of Firms in Bangladesh" Chapter 8 in Advances in Development Economics, ed by Dipak Basu : World Scientific Publishing Co., 2008.

[18]   Weinstein, D.E. and Yafeh, Y. (1998) On the cost of a bank centered financial system: evidence from the changing main bank relations in Japan, *Journal of Finance*, 53(2).

Chapter 5

The Choice between Dividend and Share Repurchase

Mohamad Jais

Faculty of Economics and Business, Universiti Malaysia Sarawak

Abstract

This paper examines the payout channel choice of listed firms in KLSE, paying particular attention to why some firms prefer to increase dividends while others prefer to repurchase only. The results indicate that higher prior income, more variability of prior income, and a higher level of retained earnings increase the likelihood that the firms will choose to pay out earnings through dividends. The analysis further indicates that some firms substitute repurchases for dividends.

1. Introduction

This paper examines the choice of payout channel between share repurchase payout and dividend payout in the Kuala Lumpur Stock Exchange (KLSE). Specifically, the choice of preferred payout method is investigated. An abundance of literature focuses on this issue, but most studies are conducted in isolation. Most research agrees that markets treat dividend-increase and share repurchase announcements as a positive signal and respond positively to the announcement. However, the studies that examine the post-operating performance of both groups do not find any improvement. They conclude that the signal is about the past, not the future. This conclusion concurs with Lintner's (1956) argument that payout is the function of current earnings and past dividends.

In studies that compare both methods, dividend-paying firms are associated with higher assets, higher profitability, and lower investment opportunity in mature stages while repurchase is associated with smaller size, lower profitability, and higher investment in the early stages of the lifecycle. However, although such studies are based on accurate data for dividends, they have encountered measurement problems in regards to actual share repurchase because, in the U.S. market, firms are not required to disclose how many shares and the amount involved in the repurchase. The repurchase measurement is based on estimations (e.g., the value of the repurchased announcement/monthly figure of shares outstanding). Meanwhile, in the case of KLSE, all firms are required to publicly announce the number of shares repurchased, the price paid, and the amount spent on the same day via the KLSE website. Consequently, these data can provide accurate measurements on share repurchase activity.

This paper attempts to fill the gap of the analysis that could not be conducted in the developed market, comparing factors on the choice of payout method using actual data. As such, this paper will compare dividend-increasing firms to repurchasing firms.

2. Literature review

Paying out earnings through dividends and share repurchasing is two of the most common methods for distributing cash to shareholders. Each method has been extensively researched in the finance literature. Most studies examine factors that motivate the payout through dividends or repurchase separately. The most important factor that influences any channel of payout is the firm's earnings.

One study jointly examined dividends and share repurchases, focusing on the relative efficiency of both methods as signaling devices and methods of cash distribution. Bartov et al. (1998) found that equity undervaluation, the extensive use of stock options, and heavy institutional investor relationship will make distributing cash through repurchase more favorable. Guay and Harford (2000) concluded that firms choose dividend increases to distribute permanent cash flow shock while repurchase is used to distribute transient shock. Meanwhile, the stock market reacts more favorably to dividend increase announcements. Grullon and Michely

(2002) suggested that the growth in repurchase activity in the U.S. market is due to firms substituting share repurchases for dividends. In their comprehensive study, many firms initiated cash payouts through dividends while many firms that have been paying dividends have initiated cash payouts through repurchase. The stock market tends to react less negatively to firms perceived to be substituting share repurchases to dividends. In almost identical studies, Jagannathan et al. (2000) and Lie (2005) looked into the financial flexibility, performance, and corporate payout choice between dividends and share repurchases. Both came to a similar conclusion: Firms that increase their payout have better financial flexibility and more positive income shock. Firms that have higher operating cash flows prefer payouts through dividends while repurchase is associated with higher non-operating cash flow.

Although most studies agree on the financial characteristics and performance of each payout method (dividends and repurchases), one area can be improved further. For repurchase payouts, the figure used in the analysis is based on estimation only due to the fact that repurchasing firms are not required to report how many shares they repurchased, the price paid, or the total amount involved. Many studies have estimated the repurchase from the announcement only, whereby announcements are simply an intention, not an obligation for firms to repurchase their shares.

This situation leads to overestimation on the part of the repurchasing firms. To overcome this, Stephens and Weisbach (1998) proposed four methods to measure share repurchase activity. The primary measure used involves looking into the monthly decrease in shares outstanding as reported by the Center for Research in Securities Prices (CRSP). A similar measure can be constructed using the number of shares outstanding on a quarterly basis on Compustat. However, both methods will lead to the underestimation of repurchase activity as, during the same period, firms may also distribute shares through stock options, benefit plans, and stock sales. The other two methods are purchases of common and preferred stock from Compustat cash flow data and looking into the Compustat changes in treasury stock. However, both methods use the aggregate amount of all securities purchases and retirement during the quarter, which leads to overestimation as the purchase price and quantity of repurchase are unknown.

In the case of KLSE, firms are required to publicly announce their repurchase activity; this information is available online. The information contains the number of shares repurchased, the amount involved, and the price paid for the repurchased shares. Consequently, this paper attempts to examine the type of payout choice using the actual data of share repurchases.

3. Hypothesis and empirical predictions

The objective of this paper is to examine the differences in firms that increase their dividends against firms that repurchase only. Certain differences in characteristics and factors might motivate firms to choose a particular channel of payout. As such, management is expected to increase dividends if firms have higher prior operating income, higher operating income shock, lower volatility of prior income, and more independent directors on the board. Repurchasing firms, on the other hand, should have the opposite characteristics, which might mitigate repurchasing firms to utilize the flexibility inherent in open-market repurchase programs. This is similar to Lintner's model, which suggests that prior earnings are the important determinant for firms choosing a particular payout method.

Benartzi et al. (1997) found that firms with dividend increases have higher prior earnings, but no evidence suggested subsequent earnings improvement. Grullon et al. (2002) reached similar conclusions. The return of assets of dividend increase firms is higher prior to announcements and lower after the announcement year. Even after controlling for the matching firms, better prior performance still persist. In their study comparing the corporate payout choice between dividend and share repurchase, Jagannathan et al. (2000) found that dividend increase firms have a higher level of prior income and lower volatility of prior income, although size did not indicate any difference between the two groups. In a similar study, Lie (2005), found similar results. Dividend increase firms have higher prior operating income, higher income shock, and lower prior income volatility. Other studies have found similar characteristics[1] .

---

[1] See Guay and Harford (2000), Grullon and Michaely (2004), and Jagannathan and Stephens (2003).

In the current study, the composition of independent directors is analyzed to determine whether a higher number of independent directors affects the firm's payout policy or not[2]. Among a few studies that examined the composition of boards of directors and its effect on dividend policy is Schellenger et al. (1998), who found a positive relationship between the composition of the board of directors and dividend policy. They concluded that a higher composition of external directors places the firms in a better position to protect shareholders' interests. La Porta et al. (2000) found that firms operating in countries with a higher protection of minority shareholders pay a higher dividend. However, Chen et al. (2005) concluded that board composition in the Hong Kong stock market had little influence on firm performance and dividend policy[3].

The Malaysian market offers the opportunity to investigate this area in greater depth as firms have to report details of their repurchase activity on a daily basis[4]. As such, there will be no measurement problems in regards to repurchase activity.

---

[2] The Malaysian Code on Corporate Governance was formally established in March 2000. The code essentially aims to set out principles and best practices on structures and processes that firms may use, such as the composition of the board, procedures for recruiting new directors, remuneration of directors, the use of board committees, and their mandate and activities. The best practices section, which focuses on making the board of directors more effective, indicates that independent non-executive directors should make up at least one third of the membership of the board.

[3] Other studies that explore the influence of independent directors on firm performance include Pearce and Zahra (1992), Baysinger and Butler (1985), Hermalin and Weisbach (1991), and Agrawal and Knoefer (1996). Studies conducted in the Malaysian market include Ow-Yong and Guan (2000), Suto (2003), Hanifa and Hudaib (2006), and Tam and Tan (2007). However, these studies only look into firm performance and its relationship with independent directors.

[4] In other markets such as Japan, firms disclose their repurchase amount and number of shares, but the timing of the repurchase is not known. The Hong Kong stock market has similar characteristics as the Malaysian market—that is, the firms have to report their repurchase details on the following day. However, studies on repurchase in the Hong Kong market only look into the management timing ability and long-run stock price performance after repurchase activity. See Brockman and Chung (2001) and Zhang (2005).

4. Sample and methodology

The sample period used in the current study lasted from 1999 to 2005. This time period was utilized due to the implementation of the share repurchase program in KLSE. This paper used the database from Datastream, Thomson Financial Services. The initial sample selection consisted of 1,646 dividend increase observations, 359 observations that did not change their payout level, 1,462 observations that did not pay any dividends, and 1,085 dividend decrease observations. These observations include firms that repurchased their shares. As this paper aims to investigate firms that increase dividends only and repurchase only, the data were further screened. Samples on firms that neither paid dividends nor repurchased their shares, firms that decreased dividends only, and firms that did not change their dividend level were eliminated. To be included in the final sample, the following criteria had to be satisfied.

    a. The firm's financial data for four years are available on Datastream, Thompson Financial Services.

    b. Yearly data on dividends is available.

    c. Utilities, financial, closed end funds or REITs are excluded from the sample.

    d. Data on share repurchases available on the Bursa Malaysia website must include date repurchased, number of share repurchased, amount spent on repurchase and price paid for the repurchased shares.

A firm is defined as increasing (decreasing) dividends in a given year if the annual dividend increased (decreased) relative to the prior year. Benartzi et al. (1997) defined annual dividend as four times the previous quarterly dividend, while a dividend change was defined as the difference between year t annual dividend and year t-1 annual dividend. Guay and Harford (2000) treated dividend increase only when quarterly dividend changes within the fiscal year were either positive or zero. Lie (2005) and Jagannathan et al. (2000) defined dividend increase (decrease) in a given fiscal year according to the dividend per share increases (decreases).

A firm is defined as repurchasing shares in a given year only if it actually repurchased the share, not based on repurchase announcement; this measures the accurate number of shares repurchased. Bartov et al. (1998), Guay and Harford (2000), and Grullon and Michaely (2004) measured repurchase from the repurchase announcement data. However, this measurement method tended to overstate the quantity of repurchase. Finally, Lie (2005) and Jagannathan et al. (2000) used CRSP, looking into monthly decreases in outstanding shares. However, this also understated the true quantity of repurchase.

5. Data items and definitions

The key determinant that is likely related to payout decision is earnings. Similar to Lie (2005) and Jagannathan et al. (2000), the current study constructs the following variables for earnings before the potential payout occurs. Prior operating income is the average of operating income scaled by total assets during years −2 and −3. Prior operating income volatility is the standard deviation of operating income scaled by total assets from year −3 to year −1 prior to the event year. Operating income (OI) shock is the difference between the operating income scaled by total assets during years −1 and 0 (the event year) and the operating income scaled by total assets during years −3 and −2. In addition, independent directors' composition is the total number of independent directors scaled by total board members; this variable measures whether the composition of independent directors affect the payout pattern of the respective samples.

The study also includes other control variables[5]: Assets are the book value of assets during the event year. This is an indicator of firm size, as measured in Ringgit Malaysia (RM 000). Cash and near cash scaled by total assets and total debt scaled by total assets should capture firms' financial flexibility. Total debt scaled by total assets should also indicate firms' financial flexibility.

---

[5] To mitigate the effects of outliers, I restrict the variables to the following conditions
 a. $0 \leq debt < 1$
 b. $0 \leq$ retained earnings < 1

Retained earnings scaled by total assets capture whether the probability of firms paying out their earnings through a particular payout channel is positively related to its accumulated earnings over the years. This measurement also indicates how long the firms have been operating. Fama and French (2001), Grullon et al. (2002), and DeAngelo et al. (2005) found that established firms are associated with a higher probability of paying dividends due to the fact that these firms have been in operation for a longer period and have accumulated earnings over time.

Table 1 reports the cash payout trend for a sample of Malaysian firms. The observations are for firms that increase dividends only and repurchases only. Dividend payout, repurchase payout, and total payout measure the aggregate data by calendar year.

In the early years after the introduction of the repurchase program (1999 and 2000), share repurchase averaged 3.5% of total dividends. This increased drastically to approximately 13% in years 2001 and 2002. One possible reason for this significant jump in the repurchase activity in these two years was the effect of the global stock market's dot com bubble. In 2003, repurchases accounted for only about 5% of total dividends, which increased to approximately 7% in 2004 before reaching its peak at about 19% in 2005. The aggregate data for the last three years of the sample period show some evidence of firms substituting dividends for repurchases.

Table 1: Aggregate cash payout in KLSE

Year	Dividend payout (RM)	Repurchase payout (RM)	Total payout (RM)	Dividend Payout/Total Payout (%)	Repurchase Payout/Total Payout (%)	Repurchase Payout/Dividend Payout (%)
1999	2,442,940,000	92,621,428	2,535,561,428	96.35	3.65	3.79
2000	4,398,620,000	148,305,995	4,546,925,995	96.74	3.26	3.37
2001	4,290,069,200	644,514,271	4,934,583,471	86.94	13.06	15.02
2002	4,605,005,000	500,119,189	5,105,124,189	90.20	9.80	10.86
2003	5,862,136,370	309,014,124	6,171,150,494	94.99	5.01	5.27
2004	9,238,420,060	689,737,555	9,928,157,615	93.05	6.95	7.47
2005	9,710,172,740	1,849,590,240	11,559,762,980	84.00	16.00	19.05

Source: KLSE

Table 2: Descriptive statistics

		Dividend increase only	Share repurchase only
Assets (RM000)	Mean	1,528,181	1,108,642
	Median	(488,852)	(572,365)
Cash	Mean	0.1434	0.0949
	Median	(0.1009)	(0.0699)
Debt	Mean	0.1808	0.2381
	Median	(0.1409)	(0.2554)
Prior operating income	Mean	0.0682	0.0249
	Median	(0.0622)	(0.0201)
Operating income shock	Mean	-0.002	-0.0088
	Median	(-0.0008)	(-0.0026)
Prior operating income volatility	Mean	0.0682	0.0249
	Median	(0.0622)	(0.0201)
Retained earnings	Mean	0.3350	0.2335
	Median	(0.3028)	(0.2388)
Independent directors (%)	Mean	0.3836	0.3766
	Median	(0.3636)	(0.3333)
Number of observations		989	29

Source: KLSE

Table 2 provides preliminary statistics on the four groups according to payout choice. The median size of dividend increase firms is lower than the repurchase only group. This contradicts the evidence in the developed market, which suggests that dividend increase firms are the bigger firms. Dividend increase firms have higher cash and lower debt as opposed to repurchase only firm. This indicates that dividend increase firms are financially more flexible than the repurchase only group. In regards to the operating income variable, the dividend increase group has superior prior income and higher operating income shock than the repurchase only firms, which might trigger them to increase their dividend payout. Dividend increase firms also have higher retained earnings relative to repurchase only firms and a higher number of independent directors. The data further indicate that, for the repurchase only group, they substitute dividends for repurchases as most firms did not pay out dividends for the past two years[6].

---

[6] A small number of observations that did not change the payout level is also included in this group.

The overall conclusion from these descriptive statistics is that dividend increase firms are financially superior to repurchase only firms. The statistics further suggest that firms repurchase their shares to take advantage of the flexibility of the repurchase program.

6. Logit regression analyses

To examine the choice between dividend increase and share repurchase, the logistic regression between dividend-increase versus repurchase firms was estimated in order to test the hypothesis discussed earlier.

Table 3 provides the correlation coefficient among the independent variables used in the analysis. The data indicate that no significant correlation exists among independent variables. Table 4 presents the logit regression results on the payout choice between dividend increase and share repurchase. For the dependent variable, the dividend increase firms are assigned the value of 1, while repurchase only firms are assigned the value of 0. To mitigate the problem of multicollinearity, three separate logit regressions were run. Each of the logit regression models used just one operating income variable.

The coefficients on assets, cash, and debt as well as the composition of the independent directors are not statistically significant in all the logit regressions. This result indicates that these variables cannot explain the likelihood of those firms to pay dividends as opposed to repurchase their shares. The prior operating income variable is positive and statistically significant. However, the result is completely different from the evidence found in the developed market, whereby a lower variability of prior income will increase the likelihood of firms to pay dividends.

Table 3: Correlation coefficient

	Prior OI volatility	OI shock	Prior OI	Log assets	Cash	Debt	RE/TA
Prior OI volatility	1						
OI shock	0.112	1					
Prior OI	0.083	-0.468	1				
Log assets	-0.077	0.049	-0.065	1			
Cash	0.134	0.034	0.164	-0.041	1		
Debt	-0.102	-0.071	-0.079	0.238	-0.346	1	
RE/TA	-0.044	0.055	0.071	0.178	0.250	-0.536	1

Table 4: Logistic regression on the payout choice of dividend increases versus share repurchases

	Coefficients	p-Value	Coefficients	p-Value	Coefficients	p-Value
Intercepts	2.9075	0.1417	4.2983	0.0270	3.0408	0.1393
Log assets	-0.3858	0.2387	-0.4561	0.1657	-0.3287	0.3394
Cash	2.3925	0.2524	3.0851	0.1461	3.1738	0.1352
Debt	1.2098	0.3404	0.9437	0.4555	0.5623	0.6642
Prior operating income volatility	33.3317	0.0286				
Operating income shock			3.0051	0.5013		
Prior operating income					12.9559	0.0005
Retained earnings	4.7303	0.0020	4.2985	0.0045	3.2243	0.0275
Independent directors	0.8458	0.6268	0.3437	0.8433	1.0887	0.5274
Number of observations	1018		1018		1018	

This evidence suggests that management in the Malaysian market seems to ignore the volatility of prior income in deciding whether to pay dividends or not. One possible reason for this is the management-shareholder relationship in the Malaysian market. Since firms in Malaysia are heavily concentrated and controlling shareholders normally dictate the policy of the firms, the management decides to pay out cash through dividends irrespective of the volatility of their prior income. In fact, the decision to pay out cash through dividends is triggered by the higher level of prior income, as indicated by the positive and statistically significant coefficients on prior income level. Alternatively, firms prefer to repurchase if they have a lower variability of prior income and lower level of prior income. Another explanation for these differences is that the share repurchase program is still in the early stages in the Malaysian market.

The retained earnings variable is positive and statistically significant in all regression models, which implies that the dividend increase group has accumulated enough previous earnings and can be interpreted as relying on the internal generated funds to finance future projects. This enables these firms to increase their dividend payout. Meanwhile, the repurchase only group prefers repurchases as these firms have lower internally generated funds and aim to take advantage of the flexibility inherent in the repurchase programs.

7. Conclusions

This paper has examined the determinants for the choice of increasing dividends or repurchasing shares. The main contribution of this paper is that the analyses were conducted using actual repurchase data. For the dividend increase versus repurchase payout, firms with a higher level of operating income and a higher level of retained earnings prefer to pay out cash through dividends. These results concur with Lintner's (1956) findings that income is an important determinant for firms to increase dividends. Although lower prior income would motivate firms to undertake repurchase payout, this is due to the flexibility inherent in the repurchase program.

References

[1] Agrawal, A. and C.R. Knoeber (1996)   Firm performance and mechanisms to control agency problems between manager and shareholders, *Journal of Financial and Quantitative Analysis*, 31(3), 377–389.

[2] Bartov, E. (1991)   Open-market stock repurchases as signals for earnings and risk changes, *Journal of Accounting and Economics*, 14, 275–294.

[3] Bartov, E., I. Krinsky and J. Lee (1998)   Evidence on how companies choose between dividends and open-market stock repurchases, *Journal of Applied Corporate Finance*, 11(1), 89–96.

[4] Baysinger, B.D and H.N. Butler (1985)   Corporate governance and board of directors: Performance effects of changes in board composition, *Journal of Law, Economics and Organisation*, 1(1), 101–124.

[5] Benartzi, S., R. Michaely and R. H. Thaler (1997)   Do changes in dividends signal the future   or the past? , *Journal of Finance*, 52 (3), 1007–1034.

[6] Brockman, P. and D.Y. Chung (2001)   Managerial timing and corporate liquidity: Evidence from actual share repurchases. *Journal of Financial Economics*, 61(3), 417–448.

[7] Chen, Z., Y. L. Cheung, A. Stouraitis and A. Wong (2005)   Ownership concentration, firm performance, and dividend policy in Hong Kong, *Pacific-Basin Finance Journal*, 13, 431– 449.

[8] DeAngelo, H., L. DeAngelo and R.M. Stulz (2006)   Dividend policy and the earned/contributed capital mix: a test of the life-cycle theory, *Journal of Financial Economics*, 81(2), 227–254.

[9] Fama, E.F. and K.R. French (2001)   Disappearing dividends: changing firm characteristics or lower propensity to pay?, *Journal of Financial Economics*, 60(1), 3–44.

[10] Guay, W. and J. Harford (2000)   The cash flow permanence and information content of dividend increases versus repurchases, *Journal of Financial Economics*, 57(3), 385–415.

[11] Grullon, G. and R. Michaely (2002)   Dividends, share repurchases, and the substitution hypothesis, *Journal of Finance*, 57(4), 1649–1684.

[12] Grullon, G., R. Michaely, and B. Swaminathan (2002)   Are dividend changes a sign of firm maturity?, *Journal of Business*, 75(3), 387–424.

[13] Grullon, G. and R. Michaely (2004).   The information content of share repurchase programs, *Journal of Finance*, 59(2), 651–679.

[14] Haniffa, R. and M. Hudaib (2006)   Corporate governance structure and performance of Malaysian listed companies, *Journal of Business Finance & Accounting*, 33(7) & (8), 1034–1062.

[15] Hermalin, S. and M. Weisbach (1991)   The Effects of board composition and direct incentives on firm performance, *Financial Management*, 20(4), 101–112.

[16] Jagannathan, M. and C. Stephens (2003)   Motives for multiple open market repurchase programs, *Financial Management* , 32(2), 71–91.

[17] Jagannathan, M., C.P. Stephens and M.S Weisbach. (2000)   Financial flexibility and the choice between dividends and stock repurchases, *Journal of Financial Economics*, 57(3), 355–384.

[18] La Porta, R., F. L. Silanes, A. Schleifer and R.W. Vishney (2000)   Agency problems and dividend policies around the world, *Journal of Finance*, 55(1), 1-33.

[19] Lie, E. (2005)   Financial flexibility, performance, and the corporate payout choice, *Journal of Business*, 78(6), 1–23.

[20] Lintner, J. (1956)   Distribution and incomes of corporations among dividends, retained earnings and taxes, *American Economic Review*, 46 (2), 97– 113.

[21] Ow-Yong, K. and C.K. Guan (2000)   Corporate governance codes: a comparison between Malaysia and the U.K., *Corporate Governance*, 8(2), 125–132.

[22] Pearce, J.H. and S.A. Zahra (1992)   Board composition from a strategic contingency perspective, *Journal of Management Studies*, 29, 411–438.

[23] Stephens, C.P. and M.S Weisbach. (1998)   Actual share reacquisitions in open market repurchase programs, *Journal of Finance*, 53(1), 911–921.

[24] Schellenger, M. H., D. D. Wood and A. Tashakori (1989)   Board of director composition, shareholder wealth and dividend policy, *Journal of Management*, 15(3), 457–467.

[25] Suto, M. (2003)   Capital structure and investment behaviour of Malaysian firms in the 1990s: a study of corporate governance before the crisis, *Corporate Governance*, 11(1), 25–39.

[26] Tam, O. K. and M. G. Tan (2007)   Ownership, governance and firm performance in Malaysia. *Corporate Governance*, 15(2), 208–222.

[27] Zhang, H. (2005)   Share price performance following actual share repurchases, *Journal of Banking & Finance*, 29(7), 1887–1901.

Chapter 6

Banking Relationships in East Asian Economies:
Lessons for Developing Countries

Sarwar Uddin Ahmed
Associate Professor, School of Business
Independent University, Bangladesh

Shigeru Uchida
Professor, Faculty of Economics
Nagasaki University, Japan

Abstract

This paper aims at examining the impact of relationship banking in East Asian economies and suggest lessons for developing countries especially, Bangladesh. In doing so, we have selected the case of Japan and Korea as representatives of East Asia. Accordingly, we have found that both Japan and Korea have positive impacts of relationship banking on firm profitability by ensuring easy access to credit and rescue during financial distress, which are achieved by the banks by firm shareholding and participation in firm management decision in addition to lending. But in Bangladesh relationship banking is mainly confined up to lending. Hence in order to maximize the benefits of relationship banking in the early stage of industrialization, equity shareholding and management advisory services provided by the banks should also be incorporated in relationship banking structure.

1. Introduction

Among the South Asian economies including Bangladesh, East Asian countries are the role model for relationship banking-based corporate governance system. Financial structures, legal system, and dominance of the banking sector, all these make Bangladesh closer to the East Asian financial system than that of US or Europe. Accordingly, this study is a modest attempt to examine the impact of relationship banking on firm profitability in the East Asian Economies, by taking Japan and Korea as the representative case, and compare with that of Bangladesh and finally suggest some lessons for Bangladesh.

2. Relationship Banking and Firm Performance

There are various studies discussing the impact of relationship banking on firm profitability and performance (for example, Fukuda and Hirota, 1996; Mori , 1994; Nam, 2004;Hoshi et al., 1990; Okazaki and Horiuchi, 1992). One finds that Japanese firms with higher proportion of bank loans performed more poorly than firms without bank loans (Kang and Stulz, 2000). Also, Weinstein and Yafeh (1998) find that firms maintaining relationship banking in Japan are less profitable and grow more slowly than their industry peers. However, most empirical studies conducted on other countries find evidence in favor of relationship banking. Peterson and Rajan (1994) report that multiple banking relationship result in higher borrowing costs and reduced availability of credit. Angelini et al. (1998) find a negative effect of the number of banking relationships for a sample of Italian firms. Cole (1998) and Harhoff and Korting (1998) find that multiple-bank firms actually have less access to credit than firms maintaining single bank relationship. Also Degryse and Ongena (2001) find a positive relationship between single-bank firms and profitability by conducting an empirical study on Norwegian firms. The general conclusion of the recent empirical studies on relationship banking is that, firms maintaining relationship banking are more profitable than their multiple banking peers. Thus the most commonly observed impacts of relationship banking on corporate firms of an economy are summarized as in **Table 1** (Ahmed and Uchida, 2008). On this background, the objective of this paper is to examine the impact of relationship banking in East Asian economies by taking that findings of the empirical analysis papers regarding the impact of relationship banking on the performance of corporate firms conducted by using data of Japan and Bangladesh and compare it with that of Korea.

Table 1   Possible impact of relationship Banking

Impacts
Increased availability of credit
Rescuing in financial distress
Reduction of risk for client firms
Higher rates charged on client firms
Corporate growth and profits

3. Objective and Methods

The objective of this paper is to examine the impact of relationship banking in East Asian economies, compare with that of Bangladesh and suggest some lessons for the latter. In doing so, we have selected Japan and Korea as the representative case of East Asian economies. In data analysis, we have conducted multivariate analysis to examine the status of relationship banking in Japan and Bangladesh. For the Korean case, we relied on existing empirical studies.

4. Empirical Analysis

4.1 *Impact of Relationship Banking on Corporate Firms of Bangladesh*

4.1.1 *Data*

An empirical analysis is conducted to see the impact of relationship banking on the corporate firms of Bangladesh. The balance sheet data of 162 joint stock companies, selected on the basis of their size, listed in the Dhaka Stock Exchange in the year 2002-2006 are used to construct multivariate models for identifying the most influencing factors deciding the profitability of the corporate firms (BB, 2005; DSE, 2007).

4.1.2 Model and Results

A hypothetical multivariate model is constructed to determine the factors, which influences the performance of the firms (Profitability) as follows:

$$PRF (ROA) = f(TAS, TCA, SAL, EQT, LOA, REX, SHA, NBK) \qquad [1]$$

After running the model by applying the best-subset approach of model selection and test of collinearity the following fitted regression model remained.

$$PRF (ROA) = 2.3347 + 0.5433EQT - 0.8469LOA - 0.3122NBK \qquad [2]$$

Table 2   Descriptive statistics (n = 154)

Variable name	Description	Expected sign	Revealed sign
ROA	The dependent variable is the time series mean of return on assets		
TAS	Total assets of the company in million of Taka	+	NSS
TCA	Total capital of the company in million of Taka	+	NSS
SAL	Total sales volume of the company in million of Taka	+	NSS
EQT	Total shareholders equity in million of Taka	?	+
LOA	Total loans taken from financial institutions in million of Taka	?	-
REX	Interest expense of the company in million of Taka	?	NSS
SHA	Percentage of share held by financial institutions	?	NSS
NBK	Number of banks the company maintains lending relationship	?	-

Note: NSS denotes *not statistically significant*

Table 2. Explains the variables, expected and revealed relationship sign derived from the multivariate analysis. Accordingly, the findings of the study can be summed up as follows:

1) Share of the financial institutions and interest expense showed no significant relationship with the profitability of firms. But number of banks showed negative relation with profitability. Thus it can generally be concluded that the effect of having multiple borrowing relationships is negative on corporate profitability.

2) On the other hand, loan showed negative relationship whereas equity exhibit positive relationship with profitability. This indicates that firms which are having higher financial leverage are to be a losing concern in terms of profitability. Thus, firms are comparatively having more financial difficulties by taking more bank loans. On the other hand, firms that are relying on equity capital more are seen to be comparatively more profitable.

4.2 Impact of Relationship Banking on Corporate Firms of Japan

4.2.1 Data

In Uchida and Ahmed (2008), a hypothetical multivariate model based on conceptual relationship was constructed to determine the factors, which influences the performance of the corporate firms (Profitability). The objective was to observe the impact of relationship banking on the performance of corporate firms, particularly the Small and Medium Enterprises in Japan. Three yearly time series balance sheet data (March 2005-March 2007) of 114 exchange listed SMEs in Japan were used as data source. Time series mean of return on assets (ROAs) of the companies are used as the dependent variable to represent profitability.

4.2.2 Model and Results

The model consists of variables that are hypothetically assumed to have an influence on profitability of a corporate firm and are summarized by the following conceptual model:

$$\text{Profitability (ROA)} = f(\text{SAL, AGE, EMP, DER, SHA, NBK, dREL}) \qquad [3]$$

Table 3   Variables and descriptive statistics (n =113)

Variable Name	Description	Expected Sign	Revealed sign
ROA	The dependent variable is the time series mean of return on assets		
SAL	Log of time series mean of the total sales volume of the company in million yen	+	NSS
AGE	The age of the firm relative to their founding date	+	-
EMP	Time series mean of number of employees	+	+
DER	Debt-equity ratio of the company†	?	NSS
SHA	Percentage of share held by financial institutions	?	NSS
NBK	Number of banks the company maintains transacting relationship	-	-
dREL	The multiple bank relationship dummy. 1 when the firm maintains multiple relationship, 0 otherwise.	-	-

Note: NSS denotes *not statistically significant*

The explanation of the variables, expected and revealed relationship sign are presented in **Table 3**. Accordingly our fitted regression model stands as follows:

PRF (ROA) =15.38 - 0.11 AGE + 0.002 EMP -0.79 NBK - 3.05 Drel   [4]

The findings of the model can be summed up as follows:

1) Negative relationship of number of banks firms maintaining relationship (NBK) with and multiple relationship (dREL) with profitability (ROA) denotes that, relationship banking does count in improving the profitability performance of the firms.

2) Whereas, positive relation of number of employees with profitability reflects more profitable firms are able to accommodate more employees. But, negative relationship between AGE with profitability (ROA) indicates that older firms would have difficulty in survival having lesser profitability.

4.3 *Impact of Relationship Banking on Corporate Firms of Korea*

In Korea before the financial crisis, relationship banking has been weak in spite of the heavy reliance of major firms on bank loans due to the underdeveloped capital market (Nam, 2004). However, after the financial crisis the situation changed and firms became more interested for relationship banking. Nam (2004) conducted a questionnaire survey on three major commercial banks in Korea: Hanvit Bank, Chohung Bank and Korea Exchange Bank, to investigate practices and impact of relationship banking among the Korean banks after the financial crisis. The results of their study suggested that, there is growing awareness for relationship banking after the financial crisis among both banks and corporate firms in Korea. The most motivating factors from firm's viewpoint were found to be chance of getting advice from the banks, rescuing during financial distress, easy access to credit and other financial markets. From banks point of view close monitoring, secured customer base, timely intervention during financial distress were the major benefits mentioned by the respondents. Regarding negative impact of relationship banking excessive monitoring and interference by the banks, higher perceived risk of banks` own distress were mentioned by the respondents.

Table 4   Empirical Findings on Impact of Relationship Banking in Japan, Korea and Bangladesh

Impacts	Japan		Korea		Bangladesh	
	Direction of Impact	Evaluation Mark	Direction of Impact	Evaluation Mark	Direction of Impact	Evaluation Mark
Increased availability of credit	+	O	+	O	+	O
Rescuing in financial distress	+	Δ	+	O	?	?
Reduction of risk for client firms	+	Δ	+	O	+	Δ
Higher rates charged on client firms	?	?	?	?	?	?
Corporate growth and profits	+	O	+	O	+	O

Note: 1. Extended from Uchida and Ahmed (2008)
    2. O = Yes, Δ = Moderate, X = No and ? = Not confirmed

5. Discussion

The findings of the empirical studies in Japan, Korea and Bangladesh can be summarized through **Tables 4 and 5**.

1. As evident in the Japanese case relationship banking is providing positive impact to the Japanese corporate firms in the form of *increased availability of credit, rescuing in financial distress* and thus in turn *reducing the risk of the client firms*. In addition, maintaining relationship banking in the form of *corporate shareholding* is contributing positively in the firms growth and profitability (see **Tables 3 and 4**).

2. In Korea, relationship banking is getting more attention after the financial crisis. Thus one of the major impacts of relationship banking is to increase the credit availability and rescuing during financial distress, which in turn reduces the risk of client firm (see **Table 4 and 5**). Also it is believed that, holding of equity shares by the banks will strengthen its monitoring incentives and would promote corporate growth and profitability.

3. In Bangladesh, through repeated empirical analysis of data of different time period, it was found that, weaker firms in terms of profitability are relying more on bank credit. However, having said this it can not be ignored that, relationship banking helps in trimming down the risk of firms by ensuring availability of credit.

4. Finally, the negative relationship between credit availability and corporate profitability can be explained by the fact that, comparatively new firms with high growth potential find it easier to raise capital from different sources. Whereas, when the firm becomes older and growth slows down, these firms start going to multiple banks and rely more on bank credit to meet their financial requirements.

Table 5   Comparative Status of Relationship Banking in Japan, Korea and Bangladesh

	Japan	**Korea**	**Bangladesh**
1. Nature of financial system	Bank based	Bank based	Bank based
2. Shape of relationship banking	Principal lender, corporate shareholding, Management advisory services	Principal lender, corporate, Management advisory services	Principal lender,
3. Positive impact of relationship banking	Promoting relationship baking (reducing the number of transacting bank) increases profitability, ensures easy access to credit, Rescuer in financial distress, Corporate growth & profit	Easy access to credit, easy access to other financial markets, rescuing during financial distress	Promoting relationship baking increases profitability, ensures easy access to credit.
4. Negative impact of relationship banking	Weak firms rely more on relationship banking to get credit	Excessive monitoring and interference by the banks, less creditworthy firms rely more on relationship banking	Higher credit level reduces profitability
5. Future trend	Relationship banking is flourishing by changing shape from main bank system	Relationship banking is growing after the financial crisis	Underdeveloped capital market paving the way for the growth of relationship banking

Note: Extended from Uchida and Ahmed (2008)

6. Lessons for Bangladesh

We have conducted a comparative study on the status and impact of relationship in East Asian economies: Japan and Korea vis-à-vis Bangladesh. Based on the findings of the study the following suggestions can be put forward for developing relationship banking in Bangladesh.

1. In general relationship baking has positive impact on firm growth and profitability as evident from the case of Japan and Korea. Hence, in Bangladesh where the capital market is underdeveloped and there is heavy reliance on bank loans, relationship banking might be promoted.

2. In Bangladesh where relationship banker ends up as being the principal lender, need endorsement as equity shareholder and management advisor. Both of these functions by the banks contributed positively in corporate growth of Japan and now expected to contribute in Korea by providing higher incentive and opportunities to banks to monitor the clients. Bangladesh in the primitive stage of industrialization can utilize stockholding by banks as a means to ease the loan default problem by reducing mangers` ability to avoid debt payments.

Finally, we can conclude that, experience of relationship banking of East Asian economies like Japan and Korea are neither completely applicable nor totally irrelevant for the banking sector of Bangladesh. All we need is to be watchful in picking up the appropriate lessons. In this respect, relationship banking experience of these countries during the high-growth era can provide invaluable guideline for restructuring the banking system of Bangladesh.

References

[1]   Ahmed, S. U. and Uchida, S. "Impact of Relationship Banking in East Asian Economies: Lessons for Developing Countries", 4th East Asia Finance and Accounting Conference, December 2008, Nagasaki, Japan.

[2]   Angelini, P., R. Di Salvo, and G. Ferri, (1998) Availability and Cost of Credit for Small Businesses: Customer Relationships and Credit Cooperatives, *Journal of Banking and Finance*, 22, pp. 925-954.

[3]   Bangladesh Bank (BB) (2005) Balance Sheet Analysis of Joint Stock Companies, Statistic Department, Bangladesh Bank.

[4]   Cole, R. (1998) The Importance of Relationships to the Availability of Credit, *Journal of Banking and Finance*, 22, pp. 959-977.

[5]   Degryse, H. and S. Ongena, (2001) Bank Relationships and Firm Profitability, *Financial Management*, 30, pp.9-34.

[6]   Dhaka Stock Exchange (DSE) (2007), *Monthly Review*, 22(8), August.

[7]   Fukuda, A. and Hirota, S. (1996) Main bank relationships and capital structure in Japan, *Journal of Japanese and International Economics*, 10, pp.250-261.

[8]   Harhoff, D. and T. Korting, (1998) Lending Relationships in Germany- Empirical Evidence from Survey Data, *Journal of Banking and Finance*, 22, 1317-1353.

[9]   Hoshi, T., Kashyap, A. and Scharfstein, D. (1990) The role of bank in reducing the costs of financial distress in Japan, *Journal of Financial Economics*, 27, pp.67-88.

[10]   Kang, J. and R. M. Stulz, (2000) Do Banking Shocks Affect Borrowing Firm Performance? An Analysis of the Japanese Experience, *Journal of Business*, 73, 1-23.

[11]   Mori, A. (1994) Investment of corporations and the role of main banks: empirical studies based on the information theories, Financial Review, 33, Policy research Institute, Ministry of Finance.

[12]   Nam, S (2004) Relationship banking and its role in corporate governance, Research Paper Series, 56, *ADB Institute.*

[13]   Okazaki, T. and Horiuchi, A. (1992) Investment and the main bank, in Horiuchi, A. and Yoshino, N. eds., Structural Analysis of the Japanese Financial System (in Japanese), *University of Tokyo Press.*

[14]   Petersen, M. and R. Rajan (1994) The Benefits of Lending Relationships: Evidence from Small Business Data, *Journal of Finance*, 49, 3-37.

[15]   Uchida, S. and Ahmed, S. U ,"The Role of Relationship Banking on the Performance of Firms in Bangladesh" Chapter 8 in Advances in Development Economics, ed by Dipak Basu : World Scientific Publishing Co., 2008.

[16]   Weinstein, D.E. and Yafeh, Y. (1998) On the cost of a bank centered financial system: evidence from the changing main bank relations in Japan, *Journal of Finance*, 53(2).pp. 635-672.

Chapter 7

An Econometric Analysis of Japanese Government Bond Markets in the Prewar and Postwar Periods[1]

Hiroshi Kamae

Professor, Tokyo Keizai University

Abstract

This paper investigates whether Japanese Government bond (JGB) markets in the pre and postwar periods were efficient. Is the pure expectations hypothesis regarding the term structure of interest rates applicable in this case? After a brief explanation of the JGB and money markets, we examine this hypothesis econometrically using Dai 1-kai shi-buri kousai (First series of 4% coupon government bonds), Kougou go-buri kousai (Kougou 5% government bond) in the prewar period and 10 year long-term bonds in the postwar period. Empirical tests show that the expectations hypothesis is rejected for both periods.

1. Introduction

Government bonds have long been one of main components of the Japanese bond market. This paper investigates econometrically whether Japanese government bonds (JGB) were traded in accordance with market mechanisms in both the prewar and postwar periods. The focus is on the First 4% government bonds and the Kougou 5% government bonds in the prewar period and on 10 year long-term bonds in the postwar period. Econometric analyses test whether a pure expectations hypothesis about the term structure of interest rates in both periods is accepted or not, that is, whether the secondary market for JGB was informationally efficient or not.

---

[1] This research was supported by a Grant-in-Aid for Scientific Research from the Japan Society for the Promotion of Science.

As there may have been structural changes in the bond markets in both periods, we use the methods of Zivot and Andrews (1992) and Perron (1997) to test the stationarity of the variables in order to consider the structural changes. We also employ the methods of Gregory and Hansen (1996a, 1996b), and Hansen (1992) which assume structural changes and test the hypothesis of no cointegration relationship.

The next section provides an overview of the bond markets and money markets in the prewar period. Government bond markets before the issuance of long-term JGB are analyzed in section three, and financial deregulation and JGB markets constitute section four. Section five explains the test methods and data, and section six provides the test results.

2. Bond markets and monetary markets in the prewar period

After 1886, arrangement public bonds with a 5% coupon rate were floated to unite many kinds of government bonds with coupons of 6% and over. Then, railway bonds, temporary war bonds, and railway acquisition bonds (Kougou 5% government bonds) were issued. The Kougou bonds were issued between 1908 and 1909 to stockholders in railway companies that were taken over. The Kougou name differentiated the bonds from other 5% bonds.

After the Russo-Japanese War of 1904–1905, money markets eased and 4% government bonds were issued twice by the Katsura Administration in order to convert the 5% bonds. The Bank of Japan (BOJ) bought them, and the underwriting syndicate constructed by 13 ordinary commercial banks and 2 special banks accepted the rest. At the same time, securities dealers began to underwrite as assistances.

In 1885, the Treasury Deposit Bureau was created and the Treasury Deposit System was established. The Bureau's assets consisted solely of government bonds. In 1902, the Bureau began to buy overseas government bonds, and accepted local government bonds. In 1925, the law of the Treasury Deposit Bureau came into effect, and the Bureau began to buy special bank bonds and to lend money to local government.

During the First World War, government bonds were issued to raise funds for armaments. After the Great Earthquake of 1923 and the subsequent financial crises, copious amounts of payment bonds were issued. The gold standard was adopted in Japan in 1897, it ceased in 1917 as a result of World War I, and returned in 1930 as deflationary policies were adopted. However, deflation resulted in its suspension two years later, together with the worldwide panic and the UK's decision to abandon the gold standard. Commercial banks reduced their holdings of government bonds because they feared rising interest rates and falling bond prices. The Japanese government supported government bond prices by increasing the Treasury Deposit Bureau's holdings.

In 1932, the Finance Minister, Korekiyo Takahashi issued deficit government bonds with 4.5% and 4% coupons instead of the 5% bonds, which had already been floated. Takahashi forced the BOJ to accept deficit bonds for the first time in Japan. From 1932, the BOJ began to sell bonds to commercial banks in order to prevent money supply growth and inflation. Bond sales was stimulated by the BOJ's favorable treatment of loans secured against government bonds, and standard price setting for government bonds which avoided banks' loss evaluation. The commercial banks had experienced difficulties in lending money, so the first bond sale was very successful. However, the 1935 bond flotation was unsuccessful.

The public offering was not fully subscribed, so most government bonds were accepted by the Treasury Deposit Bureau and sold through post offices. After 1925, underwriting by syndicate banks was suspended, but commercial bank holdings multiplied as a result of market purchases.

Table 1   Financial institutions' holding of government bonds(million yen, %)

| year | amount of holding | | | | | |
	BOJ	ordinal banks	saving banks	special banks	Deposit Bureau	total
1916	37	204	69	41	69	2468
1921	102	840	242	261	169	4097
1925	263	983	286	327	306	5015
1930	176	1315	499	372	888	6154
1935	729	2206	1076	454	1790	10307
1940	3949	5982	2609	1699	5437	23481

year	share BOJ	ordinal banks	saving banks	special banks	Deposit Bureau	financial institutions
1916	1.50	8.27	2.80	1.66	2.80	17.02
1921	2.49	20.50	5.91	6.37	4.12	39.39
1925	5.24	19.60	5.70	6.52	6.10	43.17
1930	2.86	21.37	8.11	6.04	14.43	52.81
1935	7.07	21.40	10.44	4.40	17.37	60.69
1940	16.82	25.48	11.11	7.24	23.15	83.80

Source : Shimura (1980) p.20.

The Bureau increased its holdings as a result of the inflows from postal savings. Table 1 shows the transition in government bond holdings for financial institutions. Personal investors also augmented their holdings from the mid 1920s.

Money markets eased during World War I. After the 1920's financial crises and the Great Earthquake of 1923, the markets eased again and short term funds increased. Big banks and local banks had greater access to funds, and special banks including the Yokohama Specie Bank, the Bank of Taiwan, the Bank of Korea and the Industrial Bank of Japan demanded them. During the financial crisis of 1927, call money was not supplied to the Bank of Taiwan. After the crisis, savings were concentrated in big banks and in postal savings.

An easy money policy was adopted after 1930, and short term funds increased; call rates fell and call funds financed secondary bond markets.

Secondary bond markets on the security exchanges became active between World War I and World War II. In 1922, spot transactions, which had been renamed Jitsubutu Torihiki, were settled on delivery. Futures trading with making up differences, which were suspended in 1913, restarted as liquidating transactions in 1925. Bond trading increased after bonds began to be traded on the stock exchanges in 1920.

Table 2 shows bond trade on the Tokyo Stock Exchange (TSE). From 1929, bond prices, particularly for spot transactions, were controlled[2].

---

[2] Liquidating transactions were relatively uncontrolled. See, Shimura(1980) p,117.

Table 2   Bond trade on TSE (face value, million yen)

year	bond total	gov. bond total	corpo. bond spot tr.
1915	41.9	41.8	0.1
1920	34.3	32.1	1.6
1925	333.5	285.8	33.2
1930	669.9	661.5	7.5
1935	1145.0	1112.0	18.6
1940	2215.0	1851.0	282.4
1945	169.0	-	-

Notes:Liquidating   transaction   was   suspended   during
1913-1924. Corporate bonds include bank debentures.
Source: TSE.

In the inter-war period, the decreasing bond issue policy was suspended after an incident on February 26, 1936, when Finance Minister Takahasi was killed. After 1937, bond issues—mainly to finance war expenditure—actually increased because of the China Incident and the Pacific War. At the same time, the Special Account for Extraordinary Military Expenses was established.

In 1936, the decreasing bond policy was stopped and an easy money policy was adopted. Financial control commenced through the Temporary Fund Adjustment Law. The syndicate banks accepted government bonds, but the increased demand for investment funds brought financial distress. Government bonds were then mainly accepted by the BOJ and by government funds like the Treasury Deposit Bureau. The Bureau also bought government bonds in secondary markets, and its assets consisted primarily of government bonds.

Over 80% of government bonds were sold to the private sector through marketing campaigns; and as financial controls were tightened, a campaign to promote personal savings and bond purchases commenced. The Temporary Fund Adjustment Law and the Government Bond and Postal Savings System stimulated personal bond holdings.

After the Temporary Fund Adjustment Law took effect, the primary markets for government bonds were controlled, and the conditions for issuing new bonds became less stringent. Market prices also became more rigid after 1938. Trading focused on the First 4% government bonds, the Kougou 5% government bonds, and French franc denominated government bonds (see, Table 3). From 1942, call rates were fixed at lower levels.

Table 3   Bond sales by name at TSE(million yen)

fiscal year	Kougou 5% bond liquidating	spot	First 4% bond liquidating	spot	gov. bond total liquidating	spot
1911	1.5		0.2		1.9	12.5
1925	19.1		1.8		32.8	250
1930	71.1	37.7	12.7	8	271	372
1931	176	35.6	53.4	12.6	758	316
1932	167	27.2	68.4	16.1	706	205
1933	68.8	24.5	116	13.5	465	227
1934	51.9	16.7	16.9	6.9	357	218
1935	106	54.4	5.1	12.3	445	568
1936	117	66.3	34.2	30.7	478	689
1937	153	38.6	103	23.5	529	548

Source: TSE.

3. Postwar markets

In the postwar period, the Japanese government was prohibited from issuing bonds by the Finance Law of 1947. However, some long-term and short-term government bonds were issued following the passing of the law. The Dodge Line of 1949 resulted in a sudden drop in government bond flotations.

In 1947, the Reconstruction Finance Bank issued bonds to promote inflation.

The bonds were prohibited to float in March 1949. Publicly offered local government bonds were issued from 1952. After the San Francisco treaty took effect in 1952, the government guaranteed bonds were issued by Japan National Railways and the Nippon Telegraph and Telephone Public Corporation,and until the 1966 issue of long-term JGB, these were the main components of the Japanese bond markets.

The Treasury Deposit Bureau was reorganized as the Trust Fund Bureau and its Special Accounts were established. The Bureau's funds, Post

Office Life Insurance, and government guaranteed bonds constituted Treasury Investment and Loans, which started in 1953.

In 1962, the BOJ began a new scheme for monetary control and conditional bond operations resulted in the start of secondary markets. The operation targeted government bonds and local government bonds, and it became an unconditional operation.

The OTC (over-the-counter) trade in Telegraph and Telephone bonds began in 1955. The following year, bonds trades restarted on the Tokyo and Osaka Stock Exchanges. However, most bonds were suspended between 1962 and 1966. In the latter half of the 1960s, trade in privately offered local government bonds and bank debentures with repurchase agreements, increased rapidly. The bonds and debentures were traded at flexible rates and this influenced financial deregulation, especially interest rate liberalization.

4. JGB markets and interest rate liberalization

In 1966, deficit-financing long-term government bonds were accepted by a syndicate as government guaranteed bonds. Mutual loans and savings banks, credit associations and life insurance companies that had not previously joined the government guaranteed bonds syndicate participated in the government bonds syndicate. By 1984, nearly all financial institutions including non-life insurance companies and foreign banks had joined the syndicate.

The issue of bonds depended on a restricted interest rate system, where more credible bonds should have lower interest rates than less credible ones. Commercial banks had to hold government bonds for just one year and did not need to sell them in the market because the BOJ bought back the banks' holdings one year after issue. Securities companies cooperatively bought bonds and held bond prices in order to avoid incurring bond losses. Therefore, no secondary market existed.

In the latter half of the 1970s, as Table 4 shows, bulk issuing began and the BOJ could not buy all of the bonds because a proper monetary policy was in place. In 1977, banks began to sell their bond holdings in the market. At the same time, the secondary market in bonds was built, but actually sale restrictions were effective until 1995. After 1975, JGB were issued with flexible conditions in order to prevent the banks from incurring losses when the bonds were sold.

Table 4   Isseus of government bonds (100 million yen)

fiscal year	amount
1965	2,000
1970	3,557
1975	57,856
1980	145,588
1985	229,980
1990	390,324
1995	684,306
2000	1,053,917

Note: Publicly offered bonds.
Source: MOF.

In 1966, 7-year bonds were issued, and these were altered to 10-year bonds in 1972. In 1977, 5-year bonds appeared, and medium term bonds accompanied by 10-year bonds contributed to maturity diversification.

In the secondary markets, interest rates were set in accordance with market circumstances, and issuing conditions also became more flexible and in line with market rates. Nevertheless, in 1981, the JGB issue was cancelled because market rates deviated from the issuing conditions; and several further cancellations ensued. The yield on issue and the subscriber yield also became more flexible. In 1979, and contrary to expectations, the yield to subscribers of 5-year bank debentures fell below that of 10-year JGB, and the prevailing restricted interest rate system began to collapse. In 1983, yields on corporate bonds were lower than those on JGB, and government guaranteed bond yields fell below JGB.

Auction methods for issuing, selling and buying bonds speeded-up interest rate liberalization. In 1978, the Trust Fund Bureau sold its bond holdings via an auction, 3-year bonds were issued by auction for the first time, and the BOJ conducted its first bond auction.

In 1983, the first OTC bond sale by banks took place, and the TSE started trade in JGB futures in 1985. Medium-term Government Securities Funds

were first sold in 1980, and investors could indirectly trade short maturity
bonds given that they were included in the funds for the first time.

Table 5   Sales volume of JGB (100 million yen)

year	TSE	OTC
1972	308	4,890
1977	430	136,303
1980	16,006	1,588,235
1985	394,276	20,695,496
1990	351,523	32,316,694
1995	50,591	38,462,799
1998	13,692	24,972,990

Source: MOF and Nomura Research Insitute.

Table 6   JGB holding by sector (100 million yen, %)

year end	amount private financial institutions	BOJ	government financial institutions	central government	public corporations & local government	personal	total
1965	303	2018	24	0	5	658	3008
1970	6665	16893	3578	669	31	3585	31421
1975	40983	59887	21346	0	76	9057	131349
1980	269131	42041	152093	20621	394	87201	571481
1985	564001	59790	381048	11835	923	164128	1181725
1990	708076	90011	590572	23479	941	126420	1539499
1995	1012116	202253	775571	0	621	37104	2027665
1998	1192533	274233	1284089	3451	489	46771	2801566

year end	share Private financial institutions	BOJ	government financial institutions	central government	public corporations & local government	personal
1965	10.1	67.1	0.8	0.0	0.2	21.9
1970	21.2	53.8	11.4	2.1	0.1	11.4
1975	31.2	45.6	16.3	0.0	0.1	6.9
1980	47.1	7.4	26.6	3.6	0.1	15.3
1985	47.7	5.1	32.2	1.0	0.1	13.9
1990	46.0	5.8	38.4	1.5	0.1	8.2
1995	49.9	10.0	38.2	0.0	0.0	1.8
1998	42.6	9.8	45.8	0.1	0.0	1.7

Source: BOJ.

As Table 5 shows, bond sales in 1977 increased six-fold on the previous year. But in 1998, trade decreased suddenly as the concentration obligation to security exchanges was abolished.

Table 6 shows bond holdings by sector, indicating the large share held by the BOJ in the 1960s and 1970s, and by public financial institutions from the 1970s to the 1990s.

5. Test methods

MacDonald and Speight (1991) used the Campbell and Shiller (1987) models for the efficient markets hypothesis in order to derive the cointegration relationship between long and short interest rates, and the cointegrating vector of $(1,-1)$[3]. This specification allows testing for the pure expectations hypothesis. As there may have been structural changes in the bond markets during the periods under examination, we employ the methods of Zivot and Andrews (1992) and Perron (1997) to test the statonarity of the variables. Zivot and Andrews' null hypothesis is that there is no structural change and variables have unit roots, the alternative being that there is one structural change and variables have no unit roots. Perron assumes that there is a structural change and his null hypothesis states that variables have unit roots; his alternative is no unit roots.

If variables are nonstationary, then we must examine the cointegration relationship using the Engle and Granger unit root method. We use Gregory and Hansen (1996a, 1996b) too, which assumes structural changes and a null hypothesis of no cointegration relationship, with an alternative of a structural change and cointegration. We also employ Hansen's (1992) method which estimates nonstationary variables using FM-OLS (fully modified OLS) and tests coefficient stability by means of an F-test. Hansen's Lc measure examines a null hypothesis of a cointegration relationship.

For the prewar period, we use compound yields to maturity[4] for the First series of 4% and the Kougou 5% government bond as long rates, and

---

[3] See, equations (2), (3), (3') of MacDonald and Speight (1991).
[4] Theoretically, it should be spot rates, but data are not available.

call rates as short rates. Maturity dates for the First series of 4% and for the
Kougou 5% bond were 1969 and 1962-1963, respectively.

Table 7   Bond sales (million yen)

| | Kougou 5% | | First series of 4% | |
	liquidating	spot	liquidating	spot
1912	0.7		0.2	
1925	19.1		1.8	
1926	65.3		13.5	
1928	74.2	155	42.7	33.3
1930	71.1	37.7	12.7	8
1932	167	27.2	68.4	16.1
1934	51.9	16.7	16.9	6.9
1936	117	66.3	34.2	30.7

Source: TSE.

Data sources are (1) Toyo Keizai Shinpousya (annual), (2) Tokyo Asahi
Shimbun and Chugai Shogyo Shimpo (daily), (3) Nihon Kangyo Bank
(monthly), and (4) Nomura Research Institute (1978). Table 7 illustrates
bond sales by name. Call rates are unconditional, and the data was
provided by the Ministry of Finance (annual).

The longest estimation period is for 1914–1933. This endpoint is
selected because bond prices were nonflexible after 1934, as a
consequence of a lower interest rate policy. Using monthly data, spot
transactions are estimated for 1914–1933, liquidating transactions are
estimated for 1925–1933, and OTC transactions are estimated for
1927–1933 (First 4% bond) or 1921–1933 (Kougou 5% bond). When
daily data is used, spot transactions are for January 1921–December 1933,
and liquidating transactions are for November 1925–December 1933.
Some data are missing because of the Financial Crisis and the Great
Earthquake.

In the postwar period, two sub-periods, 1972–2000 and 1977–2000,are
investigated using monthly data for the longest maturity 10-year bond,
with the latter sub-period coinciding with the start of banks selling bonds
in the secondary market. Also, the 1990–1999 period is estimated using
daily data in order to examine the effects of financial deregulation. In the

postwar period, benchmark issues were most actively traded, but these only existed between 1983 and 1999. Yields on Bonds with a Repurchase Agreement (Gensaki) rather than call rates are used as short term rates, because call rates were sometimes rigid.

6. Test results

6-1 *Prewar Period*

Tables 8a, 8b, and 8c show the tests results for monthly data from the prewar period[5]. Call rates are not stationary in most cases.

The spot transactions and liquidating transaction yields for the Kougou 5% bond are not stationary, irrespective of structural change assumptions. The Engle-Granger and Gregory-Hansen methods reject a cointegration relationship between bond yields and call rates. Hansen's FM-OLS does not reject cointegration, but the cointegrating vector is not equal to (1,-1). The results for the OTC yields of the Kougou bond are almost the same, except that Engle-Granger does not deny a cointegration relationship. The First 4% bond tests provide similar results.

The results of tests on the daily data are as follows: the liquidating transactions results are shown in Tables 9a and 9b. Call rates are not stationary, and bond yields are nonstationary regardless of structural change assumptions. The Engle-Granger test rejects a cointegration relationship between bond yields and call rates, and Hansen also rejects this. The tests for the First 4% bond show the same results, except that the Gregory-Hansen method rejects cointegration.

Tables 10a and 10b display the results for the spot transactions. ADF statistics show that call rates are nonstationary, and bond yields have unit roots. The Engle-Granger and Gregory-Hansen methods do not reject a cointegration relationship between the Kougou bonds and call rates, but the Hansen test does. A relationship between the First 4% bond and call rates is not supported by almost all tests.

---

[5] To save space, results for only the Gregory-Hansen and Hansen tests are shown.

Table 8a   Gregory-Hansen tests (prewar, monthly)

model	Kougou 5%			First series of 4%		
	exc. spot	exc. liquidat.	OTC	exc. spot	exc. liquidat.	OTC
change in intercept; no trend	-2.4	-3.84	-3.44	-1.9	-3.96	-3.8
change in intercept; trend	-3.96	-3.86	-3.47	-2.36	-4.01	-3.73
structural changes	-2.4	-3.84	-4.27	-2.37	-4.07	-4.0

Note: T-values at minimum value.

Table 8b   Hansen's FM OLS tests
(prewar, monthly, Kougou)

exchange, spot

variable	estimated value	s.e.
const.	4.68	0.22
call rate	0.17	0.042

Lc   0.09

exchange, liquidating

variable	estimated value	s.e.
const.	4.65	0.23
call rate	0.2	0.054

Lc   0.3

OTC

variable	estimated value	s.e.
const.	4.83	0.13
call rate	0.15	0.024

Lc   0.42

Note: Critical value of Lc is 0.62.

Table8c   Hansen's FM OLS tests
(prewar, monthly, First 4%)

exchange, spot

variable	estimated value	s.e.
const.	4.35	0.6
call rate	0.17	0.11

Lc   0.03

exchange,   liquidating

variable	estimated value	s.e.
const.	4.18	0.83
call rate	0.27	0.19

Lc   0.09

OTC

variable	estimated value	s.e.
const.	3.77	0.64
call rate	0.39	0.16

Lc   0.38

Note: See, Table 8b.

Table 9a   Gregory-Hansen tests (prewar, daily, liquidating)

model	Kougou	First 4%
change in intercept; no trend	-5.95*	-4.29
change in intercept; trend	-6.77*	-5.21
structural changes	-6.45*	-5.63*

Note: See, Table 8a.
* shows rejection of the null hypothesis.

Table 9b   Hansen's FM OLS tests (prewar, daily, liquidating.)

Kougou

variable	estimated value	s.e.
const.	4.42	0.11
call rate	0.26	0.026
Lc	2.56	

First 4%

variable	estimated value	s.e.
const.	3.48	0.28
call rate	0.42	0.067
Lc	1.6	

Note: See, Table 8b.

Table 10a   Gregory-Hansen tests (prewar, daily, spot)

model	Kougou	First 4%
change in intercept; no trend	-6.44*	-4.09
change in intercept; trend	-6.81*	-4.71
structural changes	-7.96*	-6.43*

Note: See, Table 9a.

Table 10b   Hansen's FM OLS tests (prewar, daily, spot)

Kougou

variable	estimated value	s.e.
const.	4.62	0.08
call rate	0.19	0.016
Lc	4.89	

First 4%

variable	estimated value	s.e.
const.	4.12	0.16
call rate	0.25	0.039
Lc	2.22	

Note: See, Table 8b.

We conclude that a cointegration relationship does not exist between long and short rates; therefore, the pure expectations hypothesis is rejected.

6-2 *Postwar Period*

Tables 11a and 11b display the test results for monthly data from the postwar period. Yields on Bonds with Repurchase Agreement (Gensaki) are probably stationary, and bond yields are not stationary even if structural changes are taken into account. The Engle-Granger method does not reject a cointegration relationship between bond yields and the Gensaki yield, but the Gregory-Hansen method does. Hansen's test accepts the relationship, but the cointegrating vector is not equal to (1,-1).

Table 11a   Gregory-Hansen test (postwar, monthly)

1972-2000	
model	
change in intercept; no trend	-3.31
change in intercept; trend	-3.1
structural changes	-3.76

1977-2000	
model	
change in intercept; no trend	-3.32
change in intercept; trend	-3.17
structural changes	-3.27

Note: See, Table 9a.

Table 11b   Hansen's FM OLS tests (postwar, monthly)

1972-2000

variable	estimated value	s.e.
const.	2	0.62
gensaki	0.7	0.099
Lc	0.12	

1977-2000

variable	estimated value	s.e.
const.	1.9	0.37
gensaki	0.77	0.071
Lc	0.21	

Note: See, Table 8b.

Results of examinations into the daily data are shown in Tables 12a and 12b. Bond yields and Gensaki yields are not stationary. Bond yields are not stationary even if we consider the possibility of structural changes. The Engle-Granger, Gregory-Hansen and Hansen methods all deny a cointegration relationship between bond yields and Gensaki yields.

Table 12a   Gregory-Hansen tests (postwar, daily)

model	
change in intercept; no trend	-4.32
change in intercept; trend	-4.48
structural changes	-4.55

Note: See, Table 9a.

Table 12b   Hansen's FM OLS tests (postwar, daily)

variable	estimated value	s.e.
const.	1.96	0.22
gensaki	0.59	0.062
Lc	1.02	*

Note: See, Table 8b.

7. Conclusions

In this paper, we examined whether Japanese government bond markets in the prewar and postwar periods were efficient or not, and the pure expectations hypothesis about the term structure of interest rates was accepted.

In the prewar period, we used compound yields to maturity for the First series of 4%, and the Kougou 5%, government bond as long rates. In the postwar period, two sub-periods, 1972–2000 and 1977–2000 were investigated using monthly data. To examine the effects of financial deregulation, the 1990–1999 period was estimated using daily data.

We conclude that a cointegration relationship between long and short rates did not exist, and can not accept the hypothesis that markets were efficient.

The reason why these conclusions are reached relates to the fact that the private sector did not have a big share of bond trading in either period. In the prewar period, Table 13 shows that applications by banks and bond brokers for the First series of 4% bond accounted for just 60% of the total.

Table 13   Applicants for the First series of 4% bond (%)

	share
government	19.9
public organizatons	4.6
banks	41
companies	4.8
other oraganizations	5.2
personal	7.2
bond brokers	16.5

Source: MOF.

Table 14 displays the high public sector share through the BOJ, the Treasury Deposit Bureau, and the Post Office Life Insurance. For the postwar period, Table 6 shows that the BOJ and government financial institutions like the Trust Fund Bureau, the Postal Savings and the Post Office Life Insurance had large bond holdings. These public institutions did not behave according to price mechanism in bond markets.

Table 14 Shares of government bonds holding (%)

year	BOJ	private banks	special banks	trust companies	cooperative societies	insurance companies	Treasury Deposit Bureau	Post Office Life Insurance	total
1910	2.09	9.45	1.17	0.00	0.00	0.81	4.85	0.00	18.37
1915	1.77	9.90	1.45	0.00	0.00	0.81	2.66	0.00	16.59
1920	2.84	20.01	4.36	0.00	0.00	1.91	3.02	0.03	32.18
1925	5.25	25.30	6.51	0.00	0.08	2.30	6.11	0.23	45.77
1930	2.86	29.47	6.05	1.53	0.02	2.11	14.44	1.31	57.78
1935	7.07	31.84	4.41	2.69	0.70	2.12	17.37	1.84	68.03
1940	12.78	27.81	5.50	1.06	1.29	2.88	23.99	1.80	77.10
1945	6.07	28.97	2.22	0.50	8.81	2.85	31.59	0.82	81.82

Note: Shares show percentages to bonds outstanding.
Source: Shimura (1980).

East Asian countries are now trying to grow their securities markets by focusing on bond markets like government bonds and corporate bonds. In order to encourage these markets, it is very important that the private financial sector plays an important role.

Future studies could focus on the timing of macroeconomic announcements—especially for the prewar period—by means of an event study. Because in the Taisyo and Showa eras (1910–1940), bonds were actively traded in Japanese markets; using daily data would provide us with accurate and meaningful results.

References

[1]   Campbell, J. and R. Shiller (1987) "Cointegration and Tests of Present Value Models," *Journal of Political Economy*, 1062–88.

[2]   Carstensen, K. (2006) "Stock Market Downswing and the Stability of European Monetary Union Money Demand," *Journal of Business and Economic Statistics*, 395–402.

[3]   Fujisaki, K. (1954) *"Financial History in Showa era: Government Bonds,"* Toyo Keizai Shinpousya (in Japanese).

[4]   Gregory, A. and B. Hansen (1996a) "Tests for Cointegration in Models with Regime and Trend Shifts," *Oxford Bulletin of Economics and Statistics*, 555–60.

[5]   Gregory, A. and B. Hansen (1996b) "Residual-based Tests for Cointegration in Models with Regime Shifts," *Journal of Econometrics*, 99–126.

[6]   Hansen, B. (1992) "Testing for Parameter Instability in Regressions with I(1) Processes," *Journal of Business and Economic Statistics*, 321–35.

[7]   MacDonald, R and A. Speight (1988) "The Term Structure of Interest Rates in U. K." *Bulletin of Economic Research*, 287–99.

[8]   MacDonald, R and A. Speight (1991) "The Term Structure of Interest Rates under Rational Expectations," *Applied Financial Economics*, 211–21,

[9]   Ministry of Finance (annual) *"References in Financial Matters,"* Cabinet Printing Bureau (in Japanese).

[10] Nihon Kangyo Bank (monthly) *"Statistics of Principal Bond Yields,"* Nihon Kangyo Bank (in Japanese).

[11] Nomura Research Institute (1978) *"Bond Almanac,"* Nomura Research Institute (in Japanese).

[12] Perron, P. (1997) "Further Evidence on Breaking Trend Functions in Macroecnomic Variables," *Journal of Econometrics*, 355–85.

[13] Shimura, K. (ed.) (1980) *"History of Bond Markets in Japan,"* University of Tokyo Press (in Japanese).

[14] Toyo Keizai Shinpousya (annual) *"Economic Almanac,"* Toyo Keizai Shinpousya (in Japanese).

[15] Zivot, E. and D. Andrews (1992) "Further Evidence on the Great Crash, the Oil-Price Shock, and Unit Root Hypothesis," *Journal of Business and Economic Statistics*, 251–70.

Chapter 8

Hedging, IPOs and Japanese Days-of-the-Week Stock Return Patterns

Ken-ichi TATSUMI,
Gakushuin University

Abstract

The effect of presence of such hedging tools as stock index derivatives and a margin trading on daily stock prices is considered by comparing the days-of-the-week return patterns between two Exchanges, one with hedging tools and the other without them. Nonlinear nonparametric time series analytic tools are applied and then a test by random weekly rank shuffling (RWRS) is proposed which makes it possible to carry out hypotheses testing. Investigating daily interpolated stock price indexes of Nikkei 225 and Nikkei JASDAQ Average since 1989, we show that there is a difference of the day-of-the-week effect due to the presence of stock index derivatives and it is also partly related to initial public offerings.

1. The Introduction

Abnormal stock returns have been globally documented on specific days-of-the-week and in specific months, for example, and called as anomalies. These phenomena require both appropriate treatment of data and appropriate tools of analysis because they are nonlinear and noisy. Nonlinearity and noise are carefully treated and possible explanations of anomaly are also explored in the following.

On stock market anomaly studies, dummy variables for the days-of-the-week or the months have been employed extensively in a linear OLS regression analysis. There is, however, a problem of multicolinearity among dummy variables in this approach. Chien-Lee-Wang (2002) noted the impact of stock price volatility throughout the week or the year on the application of dummy variable regression model and showed that it yields misleading results.

In order to avoid using the days-of-the-week dummies, there might be several ways. Less frequent data analysis (for example, week) to reduce 0s is one way. But this remedy could not apply to the daily anomaly analysis. Only we could do is to apply nonlinear and nonparametric time series analyses that follow.

This paper applies nonlinear time series analytic methods to the days-of-the-week effect on stock price index in Japan. We question "Do Nikkei 225 and JASDAQ Average stock return make peculiar fluctuations on Monday, Friday or other days?" Nonlinear nonparametric time series analytic tools by Bandt-Pompe (2002) and Wayland *et al.* (1993) are firstly applied to answer the question. This paper also proposes a test by random shuffling of return ranking to detect the existence of periodic pattern in a time series data, which has not been known in any literatures.

The nonlinear time series techniques are free from the defect mentioned by Chien-Lee-Wang (2002) and also the proposed technique makes it possible to carry out hypotheses testing which has not been executed. The empirical analysis investigates daily interpolated stock price index of Nikkei 225 and JASDAQ Average.

Outliers are carefully excluded by means of ranking, so that outliers are not the cause of the anomaly. What we will find is based on a firm background of data processing.

Dimson-Marsh-Stauton (2002) claimed and documented that some anomalies are disappearing and some have disappeared. But the disappearance might be true only after the researches and documentations on a specific anomaly have published. We will document for the first time that there is an evidence of the days-of-the-week effect and also that it is partly related to initial public offerings (IPOs) and stock index derivatives, which have not been documented.

The study is organized as follows. Section 2 reviews the literatures. Section 3 and sections 4 and 5 present the data and methodology. Section 6 discusses the results, and section 7 concludes the paper.

2. Preceding and Related Researches

2-1. *Anomaly Studies by Nonlinear Method*

There are too many related researches on stock return anomaly so that their relationship with the current study has to be briefly noted.

(1) Seasonality of Stock Return

Tong (2000) utilized a tricky method of including the dummy variables into regression equation and successfully documented globally the monthly stock return anomaly. Although the devise by Tong (2000) is free from the multicolinearity problem pointed out by Chien-Lee-Wang (2002), it is an analysis of linear relationship and applied only to monthly data, not weekly data. We will verify the phenomenon of the weekly effect with more satisfying tools.

After a framework of analysis is well designed, Miyano-Tatsumi (2004) have already applied the Wayland test and other tools to the daily stock price index data of Nikkei 225 and Nikkei JASDAQ Average from January 4, 1989 to August 29, 2003 to detect the days-of-the-week effect on the stock index returns and documented the existence of Monday and Friday effect for Nikkei 225 and Nikkei JASDAQ Average.

But they did not mention on the detail of JASDAQ Average stock return anomaly. To know how and to what the anomaly is related, the nonlinear time series analyses will be applied to JASDAQ Average stock price index data and related to other variables.

(2) The Days-of-the-Week Effect on Metal Returns

Miyano-Tatsumi (2006) also applied the same techniques to the London Metal Exchange listed daily spot & 3 month futures price indexes of aluminum and copper from January 4, 1989 to August 29, 2003. They documented that there is an evidence of the days-of-the-week effect and also that speculative behavior rather than hedging has been eminent since 1989. A merit of their research might be to study the spot & 3 month futures price indexes at the same time.

2-2. Methodological Argument

Since chaos study made clear that nonstochastic factors cause seemingly stochastic dynamic behavior, various methods of nonlinear time series analysis such as Wayland-Bromley-Pickett-Passamante (1993) and Bandt-Pompe (2002) have been presented. The nonlinear time series analysis begins with notion of embeddings, which could naturally be applicable to periodicity analysis.

Another key element is noise. Most analytic methods break down as soon as noise is added to the time series. For these respects, both the nonlinear time series analysis proposed by Wayland *et al.* (1993) and permutation entropy method proposed by Bandt-Pompe (2002) are promising for the analysis of financial time series data.

Equidistant time series samples are required when time series analytic techniques are applied to data. Most researches have been however applied to unequidistant time series data, which causes additional noise. The current paper solves this problem by interpolating the missing data, which is inevitable for high frequency data.

3. Data and Processing

3-1. Data Analyzed

Hereafter we will apply the method of the nonlinear time series analysis to the daily stock price index data of Nikkei JASDAQ Average and also Nikkei 225 from January 4, 1989 to August 29, 2003. Nikkei JASDAQ stock average refers to the Dow^{TM} index resulting from computing the simple mean value of the share prices of all companies listed on JASDAQ market, excluding the Bank of Japan and stocks under the management of the Securities Exchange.

This index covers the JASDAQ market - targeting stocks of many growing, but small and medium, corporations – which often serves as the indicator of one of general stock market trends, comparable to NASDAQ in US. See Tatsumi (2004) more for the practices and workings of the JASDAQ market. An interpolation method explained in the next subsection will be applied to this index and used extensively below.

3-2. *Interpolation*

Monday return without Saturday and Sunday interpolation is defined as the rate of change from Friday closing price through Monday closing price. Although this return calculates the rate of 3 day price change, the returns on the other days of the week calculate exactly 1 day change. If we combine these data into a series, data with different time intervals are mixed. Time series analytic tools require equidistant data on the other hand. This is the reason why an interpolation method will be used extensively in the following.

The sample does not exist naturally on holidays and weekends. Also the data of the last day in December and the first three days in January are not measured, since these days are the year end holiday and New Year holidays in Japan.

The nonexistent or missing data of stock prices are linearly interpolated in the following study. Monday return with the interpolation is therefore the rate of change from the estimated Sunday closing price through Monday closing price. Filling in the nonexistent values with the estimates, which comprise 5,348 observations, these are then calculated to yield daily interpolated returns.

The method of the interpolation is to replace the missing values by the values interpolated by the real values of two days just before and just after when there exists data. If there are n consecutive data missing, the coefficient of interpolation for the i-th value will be $((n-i+1)/ (n+1), i/ (n+1))$. Suppose there are no data on six consecutive days. Then the coefficients of interpolation will be $(6/7, 1/7)$, $(5/7, 2/7)$, $(4/7, 3/7)$, $(3/7, 4/7)$, $(2/7, 5/7)$, and $(1/7, 6/7)$.

(3) Return Calculation

The return is defined as the rate of change from the last day's closing price to the today's closing price divided by the today's closing price. This is because we would like to avoid the usage of the estimated Sunday price in the denominator if possible, since it is not the real price to be quoted in the market. We do not adjust dividend when making return from the stock price index. Annualized percentage daily returns are calculated as 36000 times of them. Fundamental standard statistics of the daily returns are the same as that already listed in Miyano-Tatsumi (2004). Nikkei JASDAQ Average daily return has lower standard deviation (SD) than that of Nikkei 225. There is evidence of high kurtosis in both series.

4. Nonlinear and Nonparametric Analysis

4-1. *Permutation Entropy*

Bandt-Pompe (2002) proposed a measure of complexity, called as the permutation entropy, for time series data. A brief description is given in the following.

Let $\pi = n!$ be all possible permutations of order $n \geq 2$ for a sequence of n real numbers. Given a sequence of data points $\{u(i)\}$, $i = 0$, $\cdots$, $N-1$, we count the number of realizations of π, denoting as $m(\pi)$, for the components of each embedding vector $\mathbf{u}(i) = (u(i), u(i+1), \cdots, u(i+n-1))$ of dimension n. We calculate the relative frequency for π as $p(\pi) = m(\pi)/(N - n +1)$ and define the permutation entropy as $H(n) = - \sum_\pi p(\pi)\log_2 p(\pi)$, where it is clear that $0 \leq H(n) \leq \log_2 n!$. The maximum of $H(n)$ is attained when $p(\pi) = 1/n!$ for all π. This entropy is the information contained in comparing n consecutive values of the time series. The time series may present some kind of deterministic dynamics when $H(n)$ is smaller than $\log_2 n!$.

Bandt-Pompe (2002) claimed that in their experiment $H(n)$ increases linearly with n, recommending a practical redefinition of the permutation entropy as the normalized permutation entropy $h(n) = H(n) / (n-1) \log_2 n!$, where $0 \leq h(n) \leq 1$. The lower bound corresponds to an increasing or decreasing process, while the upper bound to a completely stochastic sequence, as calculated in the following.

Let the numbers of embedding vectors and permutations be respectively $N-n+1$ and $n!$. For increasing or decreasing processes, the permutation entropy becomes

$H(n) = - n! ((N-n+1)/(N-n+1))\log_2 ((N-n+1)/ (N-n+1)) = - n! \log_2$
(1) $=0$,

for all n. For a completely random sequence, in an i.i.d. sequence all n! possible permutations appear with the same probability. In general, the normalized permutation entropy becomes 1 since $H(n) = -n! (1 / n!)\log_2 (1/ n!) = -\log_2 (1/ n!) = \log_2 n!$, for all n.

4-2. *Permutation Entropy Results*

(1) Presentation of Results

The results of the normalized permutation entropy are depicted in **Figure 1** and **Figure 2**. For the daily interpolated return, Nikkei 225 is much closer to the random process than Nikkei JASDAQ Average, as seen from **Figure 1**. As for each day-of-the-week return of Nikkei JASDAQ Average in **Figure 2**, the Wednesday return is fluctuating more randomly than that of other days-of-the-week. We will come back to this point later.

Figure 1. Normalized Permutation Entropy of Nikkei 225 and Nikkei Jasdaq Average

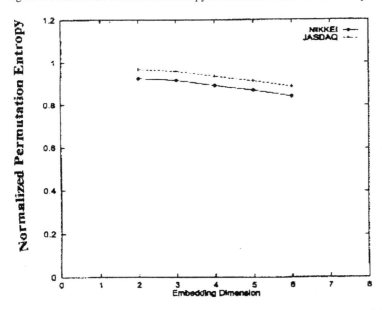

Applied to Returns with Enterpolations on Saturday, Sunday and National Holidays.

Figure 2. Normalized Permutation Entropy of Nikkei Jasdaq Average

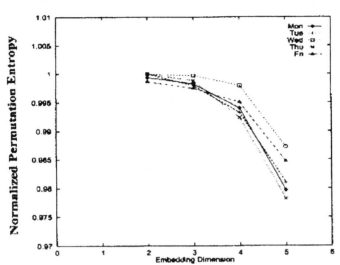

Applied to Returns of the Days-of-the-Week with Enterpolations on Saturday, Sunday and National Holidays.

(2) Drawbacks of Permutation Entropy

Even with the permutation entropy it is difficult to distinguish among specific patterns of movement, except two extremes: an increasing or decreasing process and a completely random sequence where all possible $n!$ permutation appear with the same probability. What kind of distribution exits between these two extreme is not known.

The permutation entropy can not tell the level of randomness of a given time series process. Moreover the permutation entropy can not distinguish between short run pattern of movement and long run pattern of movement.

4-3. *Wayland Algorithm — The Degree of Visible Determinism*

The nonlinear time series analysis by Wayland *et al.* (1993) is based on the parallelness of neighboring trajectories in phase space. We interpret it as a statistical method invented by physicians, but applicable to financial time series data.

(1) Embedding and Time Translation

Given a time series $\{u(t)\}$, D-dimensional phase space is constructed at t $_0$ by embedding, as $u(t_0) = \{u(t_0), u(t_0 - \triangle t), u(t_0 - 2\triangle t), \cdots, u(t_0 - (D-1)\triangle t)\}$, where D is the embedding dimension and $\triangle t$ is an appropriate time lag.

Embedding could describe pattern of the movement of the time series. If embedding vectors are close together, they might have a similar pattern.

The central point of the Wayland algorithm is as follows. *K* nearest neighbors of $u(t_0)$, denoted as $u(t_i)$, $i = 0,1,2,\cdots,K$, are randomly found then. The vector $u(t_i + T\triangle t)$ is called the image of $u(t_i)$ because each $u(t_i)$ becomes $u(t_i + T\triangle t)$ as a time of $T\triangle t$ passes. The image is generated by time translation. Therefore the change in time series process as times go could be described approximately by translation vector,

$v(t_i) = u(t_i + T\triangle t) - u(t_i)$.

(2) Translation Error and Properties of Wayland Test

The *K* translation vectors should point in similar directions if determinism is visible, i.e., the time series process is deterministic. The similarity in direction is gauged in terms of a measure referred to as translation error E_{trans}:

$$E_{trans} = \frac{1}{K+1}\sum_{i=0}^{K}\frac{\|v(t_i) - \bar{v}\|}{\|\bar{v}\|},$$

where

$$\bar{v} = \frac{1}{K+1}\sum_{i=0}^{K}v(t_i).$$

The translation error measures how the pattern of the movement changes over time. In chaotic terms, it measures the diversity of directions of nearby trajectories, therefore the degree of visible determinism of the time series data. The more visible the determinism is, the smaller E_{trans} will be.

In Wayland test the E_{trans} estimator is partly dependent on the embedding dimension D. If $E_{trans} \to 0$, the original time series process is considered to be deterministic. If the original time series process is white-noise, then the translation vector v (t_i) becomes uniformly distributed and the E_{trans} estimate will be close to 1. If the E_{trans} estimate is larger than 1, the original time series process is considered to be stochastic.

If D is less than the intrinsic dimension of the original time series process, the E_{trans} estimate is higher. Even if D is larger than the intrinsic dimension, the E_{trans} estimate may be higher because of the redundancy of the embedding space. The detail is not well known for the intermediate range of D (see Miyano (1996)).

4-4. Presentation of Wayland Test Results

In the following, $\triangle t$ will be set to be equal to 7 for the daily interpolated returns or 1 for the day-of-the-week returns of Nikkei JASDAQ Average, while K will be set 4. We will try 1, 5 to 8 week translation for the weekly interpolated returns, 5 week translation for the day-of-the-week returns of Nikkei JASDAQ Average. In the following experimental works shown in **Figure 3** and **Figures 4**, the E_{trans} are estimated for 20 sets of 301 randomly chosen vectors **u** (t_0). To reduce the errors associated with the estimates, the median for each set of **u** (t_0) is sought and then the average over 20 medians is taken.

(1) Sock Return Dynamics

By Wayland test we could know dynamic behaviors of the stock returns. First, since the translation error of one week ahead is relatively large and flat for every dimension of embedding as seen from **Figure 3**, the weekly return has a tendency to move with one period time lag. The return may have the high one-period autocorrelation coefficient.

Secondly, the translation error of 7-week translation is far below from 1. Roughly speaking this suggests two month periodicity. Furthermore since the translation error is minimized at the embedding dimension of 4 weeks, there is a property of 4-week periodicity for weekly returns. This also suggests monthly periodicity.

Figure 3. Wayland Test for Daily Nikkei Jasdaq Average

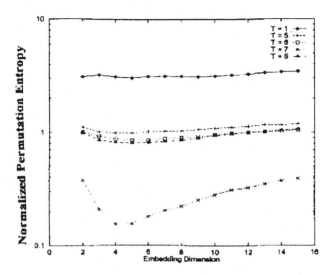

Applied to Returns with Interpolations on Saturday, Sunday and National Holidays. Δt =7, various T.

Figure 4. Wayland Test for Daily Nikkei Jasdaq Average

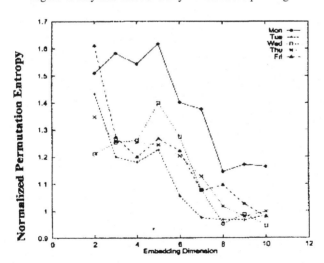

Applied to Returns of the Days-of-the-Week with Interpolations on Saturday, Sunday and National Holidays. Δt =1, various T=5.

From **Figures 4**, we see that the Monday return follows unknown stochastic process, which is different from white noise. Although we do not see any large difference among other days-of-the-week, Friday and Wednesday on average are close to Monday.

(2) Drawbacks of Wayland Test

There are several drawbacks in Wayland algorithm. First of all, there is no clear threshold of E_{trans} by which the underlying dynamics is classified into either a deterministic process or a stochastic process.

Secondly, in order to determine the appropriate value of the time translation T, we have no definite criterion, instead of trial-and-error. We rather introduce financial economics rationale here in the current paper, that is, time series anomalies.

Thirdly it is difficult, though not impossible, to estimate the reliable interval for estimates of E_{trans}, which in turn prohibits carrying out hypothesis testing. How can we judge, for example, when the E_{trans} fluctuates drastically depending on the embedding dimension? Wayland test cannot generally give any simple and clear conclusion.

We next propose a much simpler test procedure in the following section.

5. Periodicity Analysis by Rank

5-1. *Analytical Framework*

(1) Setting

Let a time series $\{u(t)\}$, $t = 1,2,\cdots$, N, be given, consisting of N consecutive data points of variable u observed equidistant in time. Suppose we would like to detect whether m consecutive samples in the time series have any periodicity. For examples, m is 5 for a weekly pattern of daily data and 12 for a yearly pattern of monthly data. The latter is exactly the seasonality problem.

For simplicity of exposition without loss of generality, let N be μ times of m. The whole sample is then divided to μ groups by m consecutive samples. In terms of vectors, $\{u(t)\} = \{(u(1), u(2), \cdots, u(m)), (u(m+1),$

u(m+2), $\cdot\cdot$, u(2m)), (u(2m+1), u(2m+2), $\cdot\cdot$, u(3m)), $\cdot\cdot$, (u((μ-1)m+1), u((μ-1)m+2), $\cdot\cdot$, u(μm))} = {**u**(m), **u**(2m), **u**(3m), $\cdot\cdot$, **u**(μm)}.

We then compose vectors by rank, ranking among the m values.

y(im) = (x((i-1)m+1), x((i-1)m+2), $\cdot\cdot$, x(im)), i=1,2,$\cdots$, μ,

where x is the positive integer up to m. The number of combination of the rank becomes m! =M. We will call these μ vectors as the original data and consider separately the m-dimensional vectors in the original data.

(2) Hypothesis Testing in General

It may be likely that we would like to know whether the rank of a specific column is on average higher than that of other columns in the vectors. Specifically it is interesting to know whether the rank of a specific column has a tendency to be higher than the overall average. Here the averaging of the specific column is taken over μ.

The procedure to test this hypothesis follows. The ranks of the m columns in the original μ vectors are randomly shuffled 40 times in order to know how often the ranking would appear. The randomness is assured by utilizing the uniform and independent white noise. This numbers (40 times) of shuffling might be appropriate for the application of Central Limit Theorem.

For each column, 40 ranks thus obtained are used to calculate its average and standard deviation. The derived distribution of the ranks can be used to test a hypothesis whether the realized original rank is significantly larger or smaller than the overall average rank.

If we could assume Gaussian process for x, this distribution could be utilized to test the hypothesis and test statistics might become that of the familiar student's t-test.

5-2. *Application to Daily JASDAQ Return Anomaly*

(1) Random Weekly Rank Shuffling (RWRS) Analysis by Rank

When we consider the days-of-the-week effect by the random shuffling approach, the weekday returns are only considered. Let the stock returns on Monday through Friday be R_1, R_2, R_3, R_4, and R_5, and then calculate ranking among them. The highest return gets the number 1 and the lowest is 5. A weekly rank vector will be denoted as y (5) = (x_1, x_2, x_3, x_4, x_5). There will be 5! =120 rank vectors. We call this as random weekly rank shuffling (RWRS) test.

The reason why we shuffle data is twofold. It is because they might be noisy, which is also the main reason to consider the rank instead of the absolute value. Second is to know the random process of the rank, since the random shuffling generates the random process.

(2) Method of Hypothesis Testing

The procedure of the hypothesis testing is as follows. We shuffle randomly the daily prices within week, that is, from Monday through Friday within the same week, 40 times. They are called as 40 surrogate data, getting 41 data sets including the original.

For data with the interpolation, we then count their ranking within week. The highest return gets the number 1 and the lowest is 5. For each day of the specific week we calculate average of the 40 surrogate return rankings and call it as the average surrogate return ranking. For each weekday we then calculate average and standard deviation of both the original return ranking and the average surrogate return ranking.

The difference between the average of the original return ranking and the average of the average surrogate return ranking divided by the standard deviation of the average surrogate return ranking for each day of the week would be considered the student's t distributed.

This t statistics has the meaning under a null hypothesis that the stock return generating process for each day of the week is random and mutually independent. The null hypothesis should be rejected if the t statistics satisfies the condition | t | > 2.02, because the degree of freedom is 40. We will call this null hypothesis as random process hypothesis.

(3) Presentation of Results

The hypothesis testing executed are presented in **Table 1**. Some null hypotheses are not rejected since the t statistics are lower in the case with the Saturday and Sunday interpolation. Returns would be random on Tuesday to Thursday for Nikkei 225, and on Wednesday and Thursday for Nikkei JASDAQ Average. At least it is concluded that Monday and Friday returns are not random. Positive ranking number on Monday for Nikkei JASDAQ Average means lower ranking (lower return) than the average, whereas negative ranking number on Friday higher ranking (higher return).

The null hypotheses on all the days-of-the-week for JASDAQ are rejected in the case without the interpolation. Even for Nikkei 225 only return on Tuesday is significant in the case without the interpolation. Although these conclusions look firm, we have to defer the discussion of any conclusions deriving from this case until the subsection (5) below in this section.

It is also to be noted that the significance of Wednesday is not rejected for Nikkei JASDAQ Average. Furthermore it is surprising to know that the level of t-value coincides roughly with the results of the previous tests. We will come back to this point later.

(4) The Effect of the Order of Random Shuffling

We have started with the price index with the interpolation of the weekday holidays and the New Year related holidays' prices. But we may shuffle randomly the daily return instead of the daily stock price within week. Although this difference is just a shuffle before or after calculating the return, the economic meaning may differ. Depending on the null hypothesis we are investigating, the procedure of random shuffling might differ.

Table 2 shows, however, that the results of the daily return random shuffling are almost the same as in **Table 1**. For our Japanese data, there is no difference regarding when to shuffle, which means no substantial difference in their economic meanings.

(5) The Effect of Interpolation

Whether or not and furthermore how we interpolate the Saturday and Sunday stock prices might affect Monday return and therefore weekly return ranking, leading naturally to a drastic change in the result. In order to solve this problem, we take Monday returns out and execute the ranking test in the same way as above. **Table 3** shows the result. Returns are random on Tuesday to Thursday for Nikkei 225, on Wednesday and Thursday for JASDAQ, getting the same results as the interpolation case in **Table 1**.

These results might suggest that we have to interpolate the Saturday and Sunday stock prices, otherwise it leads to misleading results on Monday return.

Table 1.   Student's t-Statistical Test using Surrogate Returns for the Case of Random Shuffle of Daily Stock Price within Week

	Interpolation		No Interpolation	
	Nikkei 225	JASDAQ	Nikkei 225	JASDAQ
Monday	-2.041560*	3.648944*	1.582316	8.640796*
Tuesday	-1.029151	6.112397*	-2.453225*	4.905159*
Wednesday	-0.142792	-0.968204	-0.618753	-2.054347*
Thursday	-0.368694	-1.609286	-0.710046	-2.937898*
Friday	2.459741*	-5.347454*	1.953381	-6.670968*

Note: * indicates significance at the 95% confidence level for the both-sided test.
       number of surrogates = 40.

Table 2.   Student's t-Statistical Test using Surrogate Returns for the Case of Random Shuffle of Daily Return within Week

	Interpolation		No Interpolation	
	Nikkei 225	JASDAQ	Nikkei 225	JASDAQ
Monday	-1.363798	2.468376*	1.856979	7.882423*
Tuesday	-0.695004	5.324803*	-2.131381*	3.804672*
Wednesday	-0.157481	-1.129332	-0.726097	-2.206189*
Thursday	-0.333943	-1.465574	-0.784973	-2.642103*
Friday	2.436941*	-5.774423*	1.859322	-7.107755*

Note: * indicates significance at the 95% confidence level for the both-sided test.
       number of surrogates = 40.

Table 3.   Student's t-Statistical Test using Surrogate Returns for the Wiping-Out of No Interpolation Effect

	Daily Stock Price Shuffling		Daily Return Shuffling	
	Nikkei 225	JASDAQ	Nikkei 225	JASDAQ
Tuesday	-1.327296	8.756163*	-1.888394	5.723534*
Wednesday	-0.630372	0.027626	-0.736687	-0.728738
Thursday	-0.797523	-0.023908	-0.511837	-0.274303
Friday	2.433476*	-4.610130*	2.944555*	-4.819721*

Note: * indicates significance at the 95% confidence level for the both-sided test. number of surrogates = 40.

5-3. The Days-of-the-Week Effect — Summary of Findings

(1) The Random Process Hypothesis

Since the random process hypothesis is rejected for Monday and Friday, Nikkei JASDAQ Average returns can be said to have the days-of-the-week effect, which is very familiar in stock market all over the world. The effect means both non-randomness and return difference. Further research needs to be done however. Financial economics reasoning on Monday and Friday is required, which will become our future work.

(2) Difference among the Analytic Tools

Both Wayland test and random shuffling approach lead consistently to the same conclusion in the current Nikkei JASDAQ Average stock return anomaly study. But the normalized permutation entropy shows a little different picture.

The normalized permutation entropy of Nikkei JASDAQ Average returns on Monday and Friday in **Figure 2** might be higher at first sight. The translation errors of Nikkei JASDAQ Average returns on Wednesday and Friday in **Figure 4** might also be higher at first sight. Since there are no tools to measure how much the difference among the days-of-the-week is significant, these are just conjectures. We should say that they might be so or might not be so.

6. Discussions, Considerations and Remarks

6-1. *The Days-of-the-Week Effect and IPOs*

(1) Problem Stated

In the random shuffling approach we have just seen that the random process hypothesis is not rejected on Wednesday. However, in the permutation entropy approach the Wednesday return shows more random fluctuation than that of other days-of-the-week. What is happening on Wednesday in JASDAQ? We will turn to this point next.

The number of Japanese IPOs has been increased great deal since later 1990's through 2007. The Exchange's transaction volume has been rising sharply recently, with daily turnover hovering at some 70-100 billion yen. This is due to growing volume in online trading as well as the rising popularity of new issues.

The IPO stocks have been very frequently incorporated into the composition of the stock price index and it then becomes known among professionals that the stock price index has been accordingly influenced by the IPOs. It should also be noted that their market prices on the IPO first trading day is often deemed as bubble.

(2) The Index Construction Procedure and IPO Procedure

How Nikkei JASDAQ Average is constructed will be related to the phenomenon. It is postulated that new IPO stocks are included into the index composition of Nikkei JASDAQ Average next day after the first trading day (when the initial price has determined), although it is one month after the first trading day in the case of TOPIX. Therefore Nikkei JASDAQ Average is said to reflect trend of IPO stocks very quickly.

Nikkei 225 is constructed similarly to Nikkei JASDAQ Average, but the 225 stocks are selected from the Tokyo Stock Exchange (TSE) listed stocks. Furthermore the selection is generally limited to non IPO stocks because of liquidity.

IPO procedure for investors who have been allocated shares proceeds as follows. The IPO subscribers have to pay the due amount to indicated bank account for their allocated shares till the predetermined deadline date. Then the day after the deadline date of the payment is set to be the first trading day of the IPO, when the IPO subscribers could sell the shares if they want. This procedure might be related to the Wednesday anomaly phenomenon.

Banks are closed on Saturday and Sunday, although payment is possible these days through automatic teller machine in Japan. Therefore the deadline dates of the payment are usually set on Monday through Thursday, not on Friday. In turn the first trading day will be either day from Tuesday through Friday. We now see whether this fact is related or not.

(3) The First Trading Day and the Return

Table 4 is the days-of-the-week distribution of JASDAQ IPO first trading days from 1996 to 2003. IPOs on Monday constitute only 6.1% for the past 8 years. There are the peaks on Wednesday and Thursday.

The JASDAQ market is now facing stiff competition from other markets for startup firms, launched in the past 10 years by Japan's two biggest bourses - the TSE and the Osaka Securities Exchange (OSE), Japan's second biggest bourse. TSE Mothers is established in 1999, while OSE Heracles (formally NASDAQ Japan, funded by The Nasdaq Stock Market) established in 2000.

Table 5 is the days-of-the-week distribution of IPO first trading days of all these markets. IPOs on Monday constitute only 7.0% for the past 8 years. There are also the peaks on Wednesday and Thursday.

We now understand that depending on the IPO procedure, the first trading on Monday is generally very rare and the first trading day is frequently set on either day from Tuesday through Friday. This effect on Monday is incorporated in the index number on Tuesday, as clear from the index construction procedure.

The stock return is deliberately defined as the rate of change from the last day's closing price to the today's closing price divided by the today's closing price. This is in order to avoid the usage of estimated Sunday price for Monday return calculation since it is not the real price to be quoted in the market. Therefore Tuesday return is the change of the price from Monday price divided by Tuesday price, whereas Wednesday return is the change from Tuesday price divided by Wednesday price.

Table 4. The Days-of-the-Week Distribution of JASDAQ IPOs First Trading Days

	1996	1997	1998	1999	2000	2001	2002	2003	Total
Mon	5	10	2	3	9	4	5	3	41
Tue	28	27	16	17	24	17	17	8	154
Wed	21	20	11	16	24	38	18	15	163
Thu	31	24	16	16	23	22	14	21	167
Fri	25	21	17	20	17	16	14	15	145
Total	110	102	62	72	97	97	68	62	670

Table 5. The Days-of-the-Week Distribution of IPOs First Trading Days (All Markets)

	1996	1997	1998	1999	2000	2001	2002	2003	Total
Mon	5	10	2	3	17	9	6	8	60
Tue	28	27	16	17	40	28	30	14	200
Wed	21	20	11	18	32	52	27	22	203
Thu	31	24	16	16	36	33	19	33	208
Fri	25	21	17	20	34	25	18	24	184
Total	110	102	62	74	159	147	100	101	855

In the definition of Wednesday return Tuesday price appears in the numerator, while Tuesday return definition has it in the denominator. Therefore Wednesday return rather than Tuesday return might be more influenced by Tuesday price, which in turn is affected by the IPOs and the banking customs.

(4) The Days-of-the-Week Effect Considerations

The number of JASDAQ IPOs has been increased since later 1990's. The IPO stocks have been quickly and frequently incorporated into the index. Nikkei JASDAQ Average has therefore a tendency to be affected by the stock price of the IPO first trading day. Market stock price on the IPO first trading day is deemed as bubble. If there is a bubble in the stock price on the first trading day, Wednesday return is less affected.

This means that on Wednesday IPO first trading day bubble is observed less frequently, which in turn might make Wednesday return more random than other days-of-the-week.

The finding does not contradict a hypothesis that IPO timing is associated with market stock price hike and IPOs activities are initiated when the market stock price is rising or expected to go up.

6-2. *Stock Index Derivatives and Weekend Uncertainty*

There is a possible explanation, due to stock index derivatives and weekend uncertainty, which causes specific days-of-the-week (for example Monday) loss on stock return and could be applied to Japan. We turn to this point finally.

(1) Weekend Uncertainty Model

It is sure that there are both informed traders and uninformed traders in market. The informed traders are likely to have better information from the weekend than the uninformed traders. Because the uninformed traders are at a disadvantage strategically on Monday, the uninformed stay out of the market and the market price is more likely to reveal information of the informed. Using such argument by Foster and Viswanathan (1990) we could conclude that the uninformed traders are unwilling to trade on Monday. This causes negative stock return and low liquidity on Monday.

In these regards Boynton-Oppenheimer-Reid (2006) had done successfully the related empirical study for TSE listed stocks, using both OLS and robust regression.

(2) Institutional Changes: Historical Facts

While Nikkei JASDAQ Average does not have stock index derivatives, OSE introduced Nikkei 225 Derivatives in September 1988 and June 1989 (see **Table 6**).

Japanese Exchanges started changing trading rule on Saturday since 1972. On October 7, 1972, both delivery and settlement were ceased. On January 20, 1973, trading on the third Saturday was stopped. Since February 1989, trading on Saturday was completely abolished (see **Table 6**). The institutional changes had increased the weekend uncertainty.

Table 6. Dates of Changes and Introduction

Trading Rule Changes in Japan		Stock Index (Nikkei 225) Derivatives	
October 7, 1972	Neither delivery nor settlement and only trading on Saturday		
January 20, 1973	No trading on the third Saturday	September 1988	Stock Index Futures introduction in OSE
February 1989	No trading on Saturday	June 1989	Stock Index Option introduction in OSE

Since February 1989 on, therefore, there has been no trading on Saturday in both TSE and JASDAQ and furthermore Nikkei 225 has had stock index derivatives in OSE, whereas Nikkei JASDAQ Average does not have stock index derivatives at all.

Furthermore we have to emphasize that JASDAQ Security Exchange introduced a margin trading only in April 2004. Not only there is no derivatives, short sale had been impossible until April 2004, the end of our sample period. This means there had not been hedging tools in JASDAQ, even if investors find negative news. The institutional difference has increased the weekend uncertainty in JASDAQ great deal.

(3) The Introduction of Stock Index Derivatives

The effect of introducing stock index derivatives on stock prices was investigated by comparing the two periods of January 1975-January 1989 and February 1989-December 2001 in Boynton-Oppenheimer-Reid (2006). They carried out OLS and robust regressions with dependant variable of the daily return and independent variables of intercept + the-day-of-the-week dummies. The results showed that Tuesday abnormal loss had disappeared and Mondays had started to have abnormal losses since February 1989.

These are rather straightforward implications of their research, although not the points which Boynton-Oppenheimer-Reid (2006) would like to make. The purpose of their paper is an investigation of Japanese TSE day-of-the-week return patterns and evaluation of effect of weekend uncertainty and trading volume on the stock return, and the anomaly has shown to occur for liquid stocks, consistent with Foster and Viswanathan (1990).

(4) Defensiveness to Weekend Uncertainty

In both Nikkei JASDAQ Average and Nikkei 225 we observe Monday loss. But we observed loss on Friday in Nikkei JASDAQ Average instead of Friday gain in Nikkei 225. This might be due to investors in JASDAQ taking defensive strategy to avoid the uncertainty of weekend under the inconvenient circumstance of both nonexistence of stock index derivatives and short selling restriction. It is known that the short selling rule in JASDAQ is far behind that of TSE.

The word "defensive" means that (uninformed) investors sell stocks on Friday since the investors in JASDAQ where there are no hedging devises are afraid of events which may occur during weekend. As for Nikkei 225, investors could hedge the downside risk of stocks listed in TSE at least partly by Nikkei 225 derivatives in OSE and therefore there is no need to sell unconditionally on Friday.

7. The Conclusion

This paper has shown and empirically proved the existence of daily anomaly of Japanese stock index returns (especially JASDAQ stock return) since 1989, which has not been documented so far in any literatures.

We have obtained rather clear results showing the existence of the days-of-the-week on the index: positive effect on Friday and negative effect on Monday in JASDAQ, Tuesday or Wednesday effect in JASDAQ. The current paper shows that to much dependence on passive investment management or index funds on daily base will fail and further that active investment management might have showed better performance, although accurate estimates are naturally required for practical use.

Although it might be true that the anomaly will disappear because our current ongoing researches have published (as Dimson-Marsh-Stauton (2002) pointed out), what we have found is based on a firm background of data processing and hypothetical testing. We have carefully excluded noise and outliers by means of interpolation, ranking and shuffling, so that noise and outliers are not the cause of the anomaly. It has been also denied through hypothetical testing based on random weekly rank shuffling (RWRS) technique that the anomaly is a result of random process.

We showed that the weekend uncertainty hypothesis is not the only cause of the daily anomaly. Taking account of nonexistence of stock index derivatives, short sale permission only since 2004 and the JASDAQ IPO customs, we conclude that the anomaly is caused by weekend uncertainty together with the lack of hedging tools. But it should also be partly related to IPOs. The lack of the hedging tools which this paper emphasized might support the importance of the weekend uncertainty hypothesis, but the IPOs practice does not.

References

[1]   Bandt, C. and Pompe, B., "Permutation Entropy: A Natural Complexity Measure for Time Series", *Phys. Rev. Lett.*, vol.88, 2002, pp.174102-1–174102-4.

[2]   Boynton, W., Oppenheimer, H. R. and Reid, S. F. (2006), "Japanese day-of–the week return patterns: new results", Paper presented at Financial Management Association annual meeting in Salt Lake City, October 2006.

[3]   Chien, C-C., Lee, C-f. and Wang, A. M. L., "A note on stock market seasonality: The impact of stock price volatility on the application of dummy variable regression model", *Quarterly Rev .of Economics and Finance*, vol.42, 2002, pp.155-162.

[4]   Dimson, E., Marsh, P. and Stauton, M., *Triumph of the Optimists: 101 Years of Global Investment Returns*, Princeton University Press, 2002.

[5]   Foster, F. D. and Viswanathan, S. (1990), "A theory of interday variation in volume, variances, and trading cost in securities market", *Review of Financial Studies*, vol. 3, pp. 593-624.

[6]   Miyano, T., "Time Series Analysis of Complex Dynamical Behavior Contaminated with Observational Noise", *International Journal of Bifurcation and Chaos*, 1996, Vol. 6, No.11, pp.2031-2045.

[7]   Miyano, T. and Tatsumi, K., "Nonlinear Time Series Analyses of the Days-of-the-Week Effect on Stock Return (in Japanese)", *IEICE Transactions on Fundamentals* A, Sep. 2004, Vol. J87-A, No. 9, pp. 1226-1235.

[8]   Miyano, T. and Tatsumi, K., "The Days-of-the-Week Effect and LME Metal Market ~ Nonlinear and Random Shuffling Approach~", Paper presented at the annual conference of APAD (Pusan, Korea), June 22, 2006.

[9]   Tatsumi, K., "IPOs in Jasdaq Securities Exchange", *International Journal of Applied Economics and Econometrics*, Vol. 12, No.4, 2004, pp, 537-556.

[10] Tong, W. "International Evidence on Weekend Anomalies", *Journal of Financial Research*, Vol. 23, No.4, Winter 2000, pp.495-522.

[11] Wayland, R., Bromley, D., Pickett, D. and Passamante, A., "Recognizing Determinism in a Time Series", *Physical Review Letters*, Vol. 70, No.5, February 1993, pp.580-582.

Chapter 9

Return, Volatility and Liquidity of the JGB Futures

Takeo Minaki

Hokusei Gakuen University

Abstract

This paper presents analysis of the relation among the return, volatility and liquidity of the Japanese Government Bond (JGB) Futures market of the Tokyo Stock Exchange (TSE).We estimate the GARCH-M with asymmetry model and the EGARCH-M model and conclude the existence of the volatility clustering and the asymmetry of volatility significantly in JGB Futures market. Moreover, results show the negative correlation between the intraday pattern of the return and that of the trade volume. Risk decreases as the volume increases. The return and the effective spread change in the opposite direction. The return is expected to increase, as the spread narrows. Risk decreases as the transaction cost of the investor increases.

1. Introduction

This paper analyses the relation among the return, the volatility and liquidity of the Japanese Government Bond (JGB) futures market of the Tokyo Stock Exchange (TSE). We adopt the volume and the Bid-Ask spread (alternatively, the spread) as a measurement of liquidity to research that relation.

Various discussions related to the concept and the measurement of liquidity have been made. For instance, Maureen O 'Hara (1995) suggests that minimum transaction costs define high liquidity. In such a situation, the spread is usually narrow and the transaction volume is large. Generally, it can be said that the spread is the transaction cost to the investors. The widening of the spread means that the transaction cost becomes higher. Oppositely, narrowing of the spread means that the transaction cost becomes smaller.

By the argument above, the volume is one measure of liquidity: the larger the volume is, the higher the liquidity of a market. Inferring that narrower spreads mean smaller transaction costs, it can be thought that volume increases as the spread narrows. Therefore, liquidity increases as the spread narrows and volume increases.

Some relation pertains between the volatility and the liquidity. Volatility is usually a risk index. It can be thought that risk-averse investors want to execute transaction during the transaction time zone when the volatility is smaller. On the other hand, if the investor is the risk neutral, it will be thought that they want to execute transaction at the transaction time zone with a high return—during periods of larger volatility—because the rate of expected return is high. The same will pertain in the case of risk-lover.

For risk-averse investors, as the spread narrows with increased liquidity, the volume increases, and the volatility is smaller. On the other hand, if the investor is risk neutral or risk-lover, as liquidity increases, the spread narrows, the volume is larger, and the volatility is larger.

The purpose of the paper is to measure the volatility and to reveal the relation of the return, the volume and the spread. We estimate the GARCH-M with asymmetry model and the EGARCH-M model. First, we estimate the conditional volatility. Next, the conditional mean is estimated by the GARCH effect, the volume and the spread. Then, it is necessary to verify relations in the intraday pattern of the return and each intraday pattern of the volatility, the volume and the spread.

Results of estimation show that the opposite relation exists between the intraday pattern of the return and the intraday pattern of the volume in some models. The relation between the return and the effective spread is shown to change in the opposite direction. It is expected that the risk decreases concomitantly with the increased transaction cost of the investor. Results show a tendency of countervailing change between the intraday patterns of the volume and the spread. It is inferred that the transaction cost decrease, causing a volume increase.

Moreover, results of the GARCH-M model including asymmetry and the EGARCH model show the volatility clustering and the asymmetry of volatility are verified significantly.

The remainder of this paper is organized as follows. Section 2 describes precedent studies. Section 3 presents the empirical framework used for this study. Section 4 explains the microstructure of the JGB futures market. Section 5 describes the data used for analyses. In Section 6, we discuss the empirical results. Finally, Section 7 concludes this study.

2. Precedent Studies

Many precedent studies analyzing the market microstructure and the liquidity present the results of such analyses. For instance, Garman (1976), Copeland and Galai (1983), Glosten and Milgrom (1985), Easley and O'Hara (1987), Amihud and Mendelson (1987, 1991a, b), Admati and Pfleiderer (1988), Subrahmanyam (1991), Stoll and Whaley (1990), and Huang and Stoll (1994) are some of them. Many reports explain an investor's behavior related to transaction using the Bid-Ask spread. The spread shows the cost of a transaction: the spread widens if the transaction cost is larger, the spread narrows if the transaction cost is smaller. These inferences are explainable through the transaction behavior of the market maker.

However, neither the market maker nor specialists are associated with the JGB futures market of the TSE. Therefore, the model systems used for precedent research cannot be used for this study as they are. An investor can observe past order flow with the transaction devices. Moreover, when the investor decides an own order and the price, they use macroeconomic fundamentals and the type of trading (either sales or purchase) as new transaction information. At this time, whenever the investor will deal with information traders, the investor receives the loss without fail. To compensate for the loss, the investor executes the order with a slightly higher price (when putting out a sell order) or a slightly lower price (when putting out a buy order).

Therefore, the Bid-Ask spread, as seen in TSE, means the difference between the order prices. The asked quotation and the bid quotation are put out in the JGB futures market (in TSE); then the price at which the seller and the purchaser can execute transaction is different. The transaction is done if the seller's limit order and the purchaser's limit order match. After matching, a difference exists without fail between the sales order price and the purchase order price if orders that are not executed remain in the book. It might be clear that this spread has information related to transactions. Moreover, few situations are thought to exist in which the investor can deal easily because the transaction cost increases as the spread widens. In such a situation, the liquidity of the JGB futures market is low. Oppositely, it is judged that the transaction cost is small if the spread is narrow, and then liquidity is high.

It has been impossible to use such data recently in microstructure research for the securities market in Japan. Therefore, few studies use high-frequency data. It is impossible to analyze the influence caused by the trading system, the price formation, and public information accurately in daily data. Therefore, it is thought that it is necessary to analyze it using high-frequency data. Moreover, it is assumed that it is a problem (measurement noise) to estimate noise greatly compared with the high-frequency data, even if they are low-frequency data (for instance daily data)[1].

3. Models

The relation among the return, the volatility and the liquidity is clarified using tick data of the return, the volume (DEKIDAKA) and the Bid-Ask spread.

First, we analyze what relations among the intraday pattern of the return and each intraday pattern of the volatility, the volume and the spread using the GARCH (1, 1)-M model including the asymmetry and EGARCH (1, 1)-M model; it is verified whether the volatility, the volume or the spread influences the JGB futures return as new information related to transactions. The GARCH model is general as an analysis that uses the volatility. Asymmetric volatility is included in the model because the characteristic of asymmetry is strong as a change factor of the volatility from the precedent research.

[1] See Amifud, Mendelson and Pedersen (2005).

The volume and the spread are adopted as a proxy of liquidity in this study, although the spread, the depth (market thickness), the immediacy, and the resiliency are general proxies of liquidity. The spread is a measurement that expresses the transaction costs of an investor's buying and selling. The smaller the spread, the higher the market liquidity is.

As described earlier, as measures of liquidity, although a market must be evaluated by immediacy and resiliency too, these data cannot be used.

The GARCH(1,1) — M model with asymmetry

The purpose of the paper is to measure the volatility and to reveal the relation of the return, the volume and the spread. To this end, the GARCH (1, 1) -M specification is used to formulate the conditional volatility[2]. We adopt the following equations for the conditional mean (1).

$$R_t = a_0 + a_1 h_t + e_t \tag{1}$$

$$h_t = \eta + \xi e_{t-1}^2 + \lambda h_{t-1} \tag{2}$$

Where R_t denotes the conditional mean in period (t); e_t the return innovation at (t), which are assumed to be normally distributed. The conditional volatility is defined as (2), in a word, h_t denotes the conditional variance of e_t. Coefficient ξ indicates the extent to which a volatility shock this period (t) feeds through to the next period's volatility ($t+1$). Furthermore, $\xi + \lambda$ measures the rate at which this effect subsides over time.

In addition, to verify the asymmetric volatility, eq. (2)' is used for this study. According to Black (1976), volatility mainly responds asymmetrically after a large shock: either very good or very bad news. For that reason, this paper uses the extended specification to capture such a phenomenon. Generally, the price falls after unanticipated bad news, and the price rises after unanticipated good news. In the next specification, the conditional volatility is shown by h_t as follows.

$$h_t = \eta + \lambda h_{t-1} + \xi e_{t-1}^2 + \gamma D_{t-1}^- e_{t-1}^2 \tag{2'}$$

---

[2] As Bolleslev (1986) , and Campbell, Lo and MacKinlay (1997) demonstrate, the GARCH (1,1) model fulfills the principle of the saving and can capture the effect of ARCH of higher order. ARCH-M model (Engle, Lilien, Robins (1987)) generalizes the ARCH model by allowing a function of the variance to enter the regression function itself.

Where, $D_{t-1}^- = 1$ if e_{t-1} is negative at period $(t-1)$ and $D_{t-1}^- = 0$, otherwise. E (e_t) = 0, Var (e_t) = h_t . As a result of the estimate, if $\gamma > 0$, then the asymmetric volatility will be verified. Furthermore, if so, volatility rises in the subsequent interval when the price drops unexpectedly, rather than when the price rises unexpectedly.

The EGARCH(1,1) — M model

We adopt Nelson's (1991) exponential GARCH-M (EGARCH) and estimate the conditional volatility by following specification. For the conditional mean we use the same specification in GARCH (1, 1)-M model.

$$\log h_t = c + a \left| e_{t-1} \right| / \sqrt{h_{t-1}} + b \log h_{t-1} + d e_{t-1} / \sqrt{h_{t-1}} \qquad (2)"$$

Where d_1 <0, h_t tends to rise (fall) following bad (good) news. Market participants react more strongly to unfavorable information than favorable information if the asymmetric volatility is observed in the JGB futures market. It is inferred that this phenomenon means that the market participants have a sentiment related to the investment. Moreover the coefficient b measures the volatility persistence.

Volume

In addition, the information effect of the volume is apparent in the following mean equation. *Volume* (t), which shows the volume, is added to eq. (1).

$$R_t = a_0 + a_1 h_t + \theta Volume_t + e_t \qquad (1)'$$

Therein, the intraday pattern of the volume (DEKIDAKA) will explain the intraday pattern of the return if a coefficient θ is statistically significant. Here, the sign of the coefficient demands particular attention.

Spread

The transaction cost is usually measured using the Bid-Ask spread (Bid price minus Ask price). However, when that measure is used, the transaction cost of the investor who orders the Bid and the investor who orders the Ask are calculated twice, as a "round-trip transaction". For that reason, this study does not measure the transaction cost using the (Bid price - Ask price) alone but measures the transaction cost as (Bid price - Ask price) $\times$ 1/2. The following quoted spread, $S_t/2$, is used[3].

$$S_t / 2 = (b_t - a_t) / 2 \qquad (3)$$

Where, a_t denotes the Ask price and b_t denotes the Bid price. The quoted spread is half of the difference between the Bid price and the Ask price.

Neither the Ask price nor the Bid price is necessarily equal to the contract price. It is highly probable that transactions have been done between the Ask price and the Bid price. Especially, that probability rises when the spread has widened. It is reportedly appropriate to use not the quoted spread but the effective spread as a measurement of the transactions execution cost when transactions are done within the spread. The effective spread Z_t is formulated as follows.

$$Z_t = |P_t - Q_t|, \quad Q_t = (a_t + b_t) / 2 \qquad (4)$$

Where, P_t denotes the contract value and Q_t represents the mean value of the Ask price and the Bid price. When an investor and other immediate suppliers have transactions with the informed trader considering the effective spread, it is necessary to cover the transaction fee, the inventory cost, and the asymmetric information cost. In that case, because the effective spread is calculated based on the contract value, the effective spread is a measurement including actual transaction information rather than the quoted spread.

In the next equation, the information effect of the spread is analyzed: *Spread* (t) denotes the proxy of the spread[4].

$$R_t = a_0 + a_1 h_t + \varphi Spread_t + e_t \qquad (1)"$$

---

[3] This index was used to show which investor causes the transaction cost: the bid side or the ask side.

[4] We use three kinds of Spread (the spread, the quoted spread and effective spread). They are individually presumed without using them at the same time.

Here, if coefficient ϕ is significant, then the intraday pattern of the spread explains the intraday pattern of the return. The expected sign of the coefficient is negative. The return is expected to increase, as the spread narrows.

Finally, we estimate the GARCH $(1,1)$-M econometric specification with asymmetry, and the EGARCH $(1,1)$-M econometric specification including in the mean equation two factors (the volume and the spread)

$$R_t = a_0 + a_1 h_t + \theta Volume_t + \varphi Spread_t + e_t \qquad (1)'''$$

The expected signs of the coefficient of θ and ϕ are a minus and a plus respectively. The volume and the spread explain the intraday pattern of the return if coefficients θ and ϕ are statistically significant. The negative coefficient of θ represents that the return decreases as the volume increases. The negative coefficient of ϕ signifies the return decrease as the spread widens.

Expected sign of each coefficient

	a_0	a_1	θ	ϕ
Eq. (1), (1)',(1)",(1)'''	±	+	−	−

4. The JGB Futures Market Microstructure

In the TSE, the transaction session times are 9:00AM – 6:00PM, divided into three sessions. The first session (ZENBA) is 9:00AM – 11:00AM. The second session (GOBA) is 12:30PM – 3:00PM. The evening session is 3:30PM – 6:00PM.

Two matching algorithms are adopted in the JGB futures market of the TSE. The first, the Itayose algorithm, is used mainly to determine the opening and closing prices of each trading session. The method is used when the market opens (YORITUKI) and when the market closes (HIKE).

In ITAYOSE, all quotes (orders) before the contract price are recorded in the order book (ITA). They are considered to be simultaneous orders. Furthermore, it is matched from the highest price order with a high priority level (price priority principle). Moreover, the prices that match quantitatively are decided. The decided price is assumed to be a single contract price; the bargain (transaction) is concluded with the decided price. The second, the Zaraba algorithm, is used during trading sessions to match orders continuously under price priority and time precedence principles. This is a method used in the transaction time other than opening and closing. After the opening price is decided, this Zaraba method is used until the closing price is decided. The bargain is individually concluded on a first-come-first-served basis during the transaction session; many contract prices are decided continuously.

All JGB futures transactions are executed in accordance with the auction market principle: price priority and time precedence.

5. Data

This section presents a description of the data used for analyses. This study uses high-frequency data of the JGB futures to examine the characteristics of the intraday pattern of volatility. The sample period is April 1, 2003 – March 31, 2004. The sample period has 245 transaction business days. Furthermore, there are 426 samples in one business day; in all, the samples are 104370^5.

The data are obtained from "KIKKEI NEEDS (Tick Saiken Sakimono Option)". The return of JGB futures is calculated for every interval. First, the contract price data are made. The contract price of the interval immediately before that is used when transactions are not contracted at a certain interval and the contract price has not been described in the book (ITA). This means that new information has not been brought to the market. The quotes are also similar. In addition, as for the quotes, we have selected the combination of the Bid price and the Ask price immediately before the transaction is made.

According to Huang and Stoll (1996), spreads of three kinds are used in this study. These are the spread, the quote spread, and the effective spread.

---

[5] However, the market is open only in the morning (Zenba) on December 30, 2003 and January 5, 2004. Therefore, these two transaction days were excluded from the sample. Moreover, one interval is one minute. For instance, in the first session (Zaraba), it is divided as follows, 9:00–9:01, 9:01–9:02, … ,10:59–11:00.

The correlation between the volatility and the volume isn't strong, although the respective correlations of time series data are shown in Table 2. Furthermore, the correlation of volatility and the three spreads isn't strong. Next, the correlation of the volume and the spread isn't also strong. A problem of multicollinearity would probably not arise even if they were used simultaneously for estimation.

Moreover, when R (return) was checked using the Box–Jenkins method, the auto-correlation is admitted in the squared residuals from the ACF coefficient, the PACF coefficient, and the Q statistic in this paper. There is no unit root by the unit root tests of the ADF and the PP.

Table 1 Statistics of variables

	Price	Return	Volume	Spread	Quoted Spread	Effective Spread
Mean	13994.972	-0.000038	14.442608	1.29607167	0.648035834	0.631211076
Standard deviation	265.72857	0.0153607	126.58615	1.5650212	0.7825106	0.71528027
Variance	70611.673	0.00023595	16024.054	2.44929135	0.612322839	0.511625865
Kurtosis	-1.039902	311.625424	860.91898	1401.26026	1401.260257	1505.778667
Skewness	0.4178135	-3.1118635	24.602158	31.3864273	31.3864273	30.45679327
Observations	104370	104370	104370	104370	104370	104370

Table 2 Correlation

	Price	Return	Volume	Spread	Quoted Spread	Effective Spread
Price	1					
Return	0.0037	1				
Volume	0.0022	-0.0164	1			
Spread	-0.0996	0.0292	0.1768	1		
Quoted Spread	-0.0996	0.0292	0.1768	1	1	
Effective Spread	-0.1077	-0.0409	0.2102	0.6428	0.6428	1

6. Empirical Results

From the results of the GARCH (1,1)-M with asymmetry and the EGARCH(1,1)-M model expressed in Table 3, the intraday pattern of the volatility explains the intraday pattern of the return. The coefficients

a_1 of that are significant and negative, contrary to our expectation. The coefficient γ is positive significantly and the coefficient d is negative significantly, the asymmetry of volatility is verified. Moreover, the coefficient ξ, λ and b measures the volatility persistence, they are positive significantly. The volatility crusting is verified too. That is the fact that different shock is likely to be followed by other shock of the same sign.

The coefficient θ of that is significant and negative when the volume is an explanatory variable in the EGARCH (1, 1)-M model (Table 4). This result implies that risk decreases as the volume increases. But from the result of GARCH (1, 1)-M with asymmetry, the coefficient θ is positive. This result implies that risk increases as the volume increases. Moreover, the asymmetry of volatility and the volatility crusting are verified.

The coefficients ϕ of those are significant and positive when the spread (the spread and the quoted spread) is an independent variable in Table 5, 6. However in table7, the coefficient of effective spread is negative significantly in GARCH (1, 1)-M with asymmetry model and EGARCH (1, 1)-M model. The return is expected to decrease, as the spread widens. This result implies that risk decreases as the spread widens. Moreover, the asymmetry of volatility and the volatility crusting are verified in every three spread models. Those results correspond to the results of Table 3, 4.

Table 3 Estimation GARCH(1,1)-M with asymmetry and EGARCH(1,1)-M

	GARCH-M with asymmetry			EGARCH-M	
Variable	Coeff	Signif	Variable	Coeff	Signif
1. a_0	7.61E-05	0.0051	1. a_0	-0.0035	0
2. a_1	-0.3521	0.0003	2. a_1	-0.0003	0
3. η	7.33E-06	0	3. c	-1.2701	0
4. ξ	0.342	0	4. a	0.5492	0
5. λ	0.7551	0	5. b	0.8856	0
6. γ	0.1462	0	6. d	-0.0566	0
Log Likelihood	312659.4674		Log Likelihood	313156.3483	

* Significance = P value

Table 4 Volume

Variable	GARCH-M with asymmetry Coeff	Signif	Variable	EGARCH-M Coeff	Signif
1. a_0	7.57E-05	0	1. a_0	-0.0035	0
2. a_1	-0.3524	0	2. a_1	-0.0003	0
3. θ	6.06E-08	0.0008	3. θ	-0.0000007	0
4. η	7.33E-06	0	4. c	-1.2774	0
5. ξ	0.3419	0	5. a	0.5518	0
6. λ	0.7551	0	6. b	0.8849	0
7. γ	0.1464	0	7. d	-0.0576	0
Log Likelihood	312659.4921		Log Likelihood	313159.8322	

*θ= the coefficient of Volume.

Table 5 Spread

Variable	GARCH-M with asymmetry Coeff	Signif	Variable	EGARCH-M Coeff	Signif
1. a_0	-1.98E-03	0	1. a_0	0.00001	0.8612
2. a_1	-0.9689	0	2. a_1	0.00016	0
3. $\varphi(S)$	2.00E-03	0	3. $\varphi(S)$	0.0017	0
4. η	4.63E-06	0	4. c	-1.0757	0
5. ξ	0.2597	0	5. a	0.4993	0
6. λ	0.7728	0	6. b	0.9071	0
7. γ	0.322	0	7. d	-0.0927	0
Log Likelihood	313593.0123		Log Likelihood	314961.4503	

* $\phi(S)$= the coefficient of Spread

In Table 8, 9, 10, we estimate the equations (1)''' for the conditional mean. These results correspond to results of the model described above. When the volume and the spread are added to the equations (1), the coefficient of the volume is significant and negative in GARCH (1,1)-M with asymmetry model and EGARCH (1, 1)-M model. This result implies that risk decreases as the volume increases. The coefficients ϕ of the spread and the quoted spread are significant and positive in the conditional mean equations (1)' and (1)''. This result is consistent with the results of

Table 5 and Table 6. However, from the result of the equation (1)''', the coefficient ϕ of the effective spread is significant and negative. This result shows that the return decreases as the spread widens. In a word, the bigger the transaction cost, the lesser the return. This result implies that risk decreases as the spread widens. As the coefficient θ and ϕ show, there is a tendency of countervailing change between the intraday patterns of the volume and the spread.

Table 6 Quoted Spread

	GARCH-M with asymmetry			EGARCH-M	
Variable	Coeff	Signif	Variable	Coeff	Signif
1. a_0	-1.98E-03	0	1. a_0	-0.0001	0.3314
2. a_1	-0.9689	0	2. a_1	0.0002	0
3. ϕ(QS)	4.00E-03	0	3. ϕ(QS)	0.0035	0
4. η	4.63E-06	0	4. c	-1.0735	0
5. ξ	0.2597	0	5. a	0.4986	0
6. λ	0.7728	0	6. b	0.9073	0
7. γ	0.322	0	7. d	-0.0932	0
Log Likelihood	313593.0123		Log Likelihood	314961.7779	

* ϕ(QS) = the coefficient of Quoted Spread

Table 7 Effective Spread

	GARCH-M with asymmetry			EGARCH-M	
Variable	Coeff	Signif	Variable	Coeff	Signif
1. a_0	1.76E-03	0	1. a_0	0.0021	0
2. a_1	0.5848	0	2. a_1	-2.80E-06	0
3. φ(ES)	-3.56E-03	0	3. φ(ES)	-0.0042	0
4. η	6.28E-06	0	4. c	-1.1154	0
5. ξ	0.3818	0	5. a	0.5139	0
6. λ	0.7681	0	6. b	0.9028	0
7. γ	6.77E-03	0	7. d	0.0210	0
Log Likelihood	313533.3577		Log Likelihood	315295.5109	

* ϕ(QS) = the coefficient of Effective Spread

Table 8 Volume and Spread

GARCH-M with asymmetry			EGARCH-M		
Variable	Coeff	Signif	Variable	Coeff	Signif
1. a_0	-2.10E-03	0	1. a_0	-0.0004	0
2. a_1	-0.9965	0	2. a_1	0.00014	0
3. θ	-3.26E-06	0	3. θ	-2.89E-06	0
4. $\phi(S)$	2.14E-03	0	4. $\phi(S)$	0.0019	0
5. η	4.69E-06	0	5. c	-1.0622	0
6. ξ	0.2515	0	6. a	0.4908	0
7. λ	0.7736	0	7. b	0.9082	0
8. γ	0.3249	0	8. d	-0.0963	0
Log Likelihood	313659.8006		Log Likelihood	315015.5496	

* θ = the coefficient of Volume., $\phi(S)$ = the coefficient of Spread

Table 9 Volume and Quoted Spread

GARCH-M with asymmetry			EGARCH-M		
Variable	Coeff	Signif	Variable	Coeff	Signif
1. a_0	-2.10E-03	0	1. a_0	-0.0004	1E-06
2. a_1	-0.9965	0	2. a_1	0.0001	0
3. θ	-3.26E-06	0	3. θ	-2.9E-06	0
4. $\phi(QS)$	4.27E-03	0	4. $\phi(QS)$	0.0038	0
5. η	4.69E-06	0	5. c	-1.0621	0
6. ξ	0.2515	0	6. a	0.4908	0
7. λ	0.7736	0	7. b	0.9082	0
8. γ	0.3249	0	8. d	-0.0963	0
Log Likelihood	313659.8006		Log Likelihood	315015.55	

*θ = the coefficient of Volume., $\phi(QS)$ = the coefficient of Quoted Spread

Moreover, the asymmetric volatility is confirmed significantly except for the result of Table10. The effect of ARCH and the effect of GARCH are significant; also, the effect of shocks continues for a long term.

In Table 9, when the volume and the quoted spread are added to the equations (1), the coefficient of the volume is significant and negative in GARCH (1, 1)-M with asymmetry model. But from the result of EGARCH (1, 1)-M, the coefficient θ is positive. This result is consistent with the result Table 8. The coefficient ϕ of the quoted spread is significant and positive in the conditional mean equations (1)". This result shows that the return increases as the spread widens. Furthermore, the asymmetry of volatility and the volatility crusting are verified.

In Table 10, when the volume and the effective spread are added to the equations (1), the coefficient θ of the volume is significant and positive in GARCH (1, 1)-M with asymmetry model and EGARCH (1, 1)-M model. The correlation between the return and the volume is positive. This result implies that risk increases as the volume increases. The coefficient ϕ of the effective spread is significant and negative in the conditional mean equations (1)"'. This result shows that the return decreases as the spread widens. The volatility crusting is verified.

From the above estimation results, the coefficient θ of the volume is negative. The correlation between the return and the volume is negative. In a word, the intraday pattern of the volatility and the intraday pattern of the volume change are in the opposite direction. The coefficient of the effective spread is negative. The correlation between the return and the spread is negative. The intraday pattern of the effective spread and the intraday pattern of the volatility change in the opposite direction. This relation shows that the spread widens; then the volatility decreases.

Table 10 Volume and Effective Spread

GARCH-M with asymmetry			EGARCH-M		
Variable	Coeff	Signif	Variable	Coeff	Signif
1. a_0	1.90E-03	0	1. a_0	0.0025	0
2. a_1	0.6617	0	2. a_1	0.00003	0
3. θ	3.55E-06	0	3. θ	4.94E-06	0
4. ϕ (ES)	-3.90E-03	0	4. ϕ (ES)	-0.0046	0
5. η	5.97E-06	0	5. c	-1.0831	0
6. ξ	0.3815	0	6. a	0.5080	0
7. λ	0.7722	0	7. b	0.9063	0
8. γ	-3.88E-03	0.0010	8. d	0.0270	0
Log Likelihood	313617.3788		Log Likelihood	315440.4607	

$*\theta$ = the coefficient of Volume., ϕ (ES) = the coefficient of Effective Spread

Results described above show that, with regard to the persistence of volatility, the persistence lasts. The effect of ARCH and the effect of GARCH are significant; also, the effect of shocks continues for a long term. Regarding the asymmetric volatility, this is confirmed significantly. Market participants react more strongly to unfavorable information than favorable information. It is inferred that this phenomenon means that the market participants have a sentiment related to the investment.

7. Conclusion

This paper analyses the relation among the return, the volatility and liquidity of the Japanese Government Bond (JGB) futures market of the Tokyo Stock Exchange (TSE). The purpose is to measure the volatility and to reveal the relation of the return, the volume and the spread. To this end, it is necessary to verify the relations in the intraday pattern of the return and each intraday pattern of the volatility, the volume and the spread. Then, we estimate the GARCH (1, 1)-M with asymmetry model and the EGARCH (1, 1)-M model.

Results of estimation show that an opposite relation exists between the intraday pattern of the return and the intraday pattern of the volume in some models. The negative coefficient of the volume represents that the return decreases as the volume increases. This result implies that risk decreases as the volume increases. Moreover, the relation between the return and the effective spread is shown to change in the opposite direction. The negative coefficient of the spread signifies the return decrease as the spread widens. This result implies that risk decreases as the effective spread increases. It is expected that the risk decreases concomitantly with the increased transaction cost of the investor. Results show a tendency of countervailing change between the intraday patterns of the volume and the spread.

Regarding the persistence of volatility, the effect of ARCH and the effect of GARCH are significant; also, the effect of shocks continues for a long term. Regarding the asymmetric volatility, this is confirmed significantly. Market participants react more strongly to unfavorable information than favorable information. It is inferred that this phenomenon means that the market participants have a sentiment related to the investment. Therefore, irrationality (illogical behavior) exists in an investor's transaction behavior.

References

[1] Admati, A., and P. Pfleiderer (1988) "A Theory of Intraday Trading Patterns," *Review of Financial Studies* 1, 3-40.

[2] Amihud,Y., and H. Mendelson [1987] "Trading Mechanisms and Stock Returns: An Empirical Investigation," *Journal of Finance* 42, 533-553.

[3] Amihud,Y., and H. Mendelson [1991a] "Market Microstructure and Price Discovery on the Tokyo Stock Exchange," in *Japanese Financial Market Research* edited by W. T. Ziemba. 169-196.

[4] Amihud,Y., and H. Mendelson [1991b] "Volatility, Efficiency, and Trading: Evidence from the Japanese Stock Market," *Journal of Finance* 46, 1765-1789.

[5] Amihud,Y., and H. Mendelson [2005] Liquidity and Asset Pricest, Foundation and Trends in Finance ,Volume 1 Issue 4 .

[6] Black, F. [1976]" Studies of Stock Market Volatility Changes,"1976 Proceedings of the American Statistical Association, Business and Economics Statistic Section, 177-181.

[7] Bollerslev, T. [1986] "Generalized autoregressive conditional heteroskedasticity," *Journal of Econometrics*, 31, 307-327.

[8] Campbell, J., Lo, A., & MacKinlay, A. [1997] The Econometrics of Financial Markets, Princeton University Press.

[9] Copeland, T., and D. Galai [1983] "Information Effects on the Bid-Ask Spread,"*Journal of Finance* 38, 1457-1469.

[10] Easley, D., and O'Hara, M. [1987] "Price, Trading Size, and Information in Securities Markets,"*Jorunal of Financial Economics* 19, 69-90.

[11] Engle, R., D. M. Lilien, and R. P. Robons [1987] "Estimating Time Varying Risk Premia in the Term Structure: the ARCH-M Model." Econometrica 55, 391-407.

[12] Graman,M.B.[1976] "Market microstructure," *Journal of Financial Economics* 3, 257-275.

[13] Glosten, L., and P. Milgrom [1985] "Bid, Ask and Transaction Prices in a Specialist Market with Heterogeneously Informed Traders, "*Journal of Financial Economics* 14, 465-474.

[14] Huang, R., and Stoll, H [1994] "Market Microstructure and Stock Return Predictions," *The Review of Financial Studies* 7, 179-213.

[15] Huang, R., and Stoll, H [1996] "Dealer versus auction markets: A paired comparison of execution costs on NASDAQ and the NYSE," *Journal of Financial Economics* 41, 313-357.

[16] Nelson, D. B. [1991] "Conditional Heteroskedasticity in Asset Returns; A New Approach", *Econometrica* 59, 347-370.

[17] O'Hara, M. [1996] *Market Microstructure Theory,* Blackwell Publishers .

[18] Subrahmanyam, A. [1991] "Risk Aversion, Market Liquidity, and Price Efficiency," *Review of Financial Studies* 4, 417-442.

[19] Stoll,H. R. and R. E. Whaley [1990] "Stock Market Structure and Volatility," *Review of Financial Studies* 3, 37-71.

Chapter 10

Consistency of Risk Attitude and other Investment Behavior of Japanese Fund Managers

Masayuki Susai
Nagasaki University

Hiroshi Moriyasu
Nagasaki University

Abstract

In this paper, we investigate risk consistency and other investment behaviors of fund managers working at Japanese investment institutions using a questionnaire based survey that was conducted in October of 2005. In particular, we focused on the herding behavior and disposition effect of fund managers. We found that 'risk inconsistent' fund managers have a tendency to show disposition behavior. As for herding behavior, we could not find any strong evidence that might indicate a difference between the two groups.

1. Introduction

Recently, a substantial number of papers have investigated the behavioral characteristics of investors based on research results from within the field of behavioral finance. In addition to theoretical analysis, empirical research has been aggressively carried out using both market data as well as information on individual investors. Within this vast research, a variety of behavioral characteristics have been found in investors that match characteristics implicated in behavioral finance studies.

Suto and Toshino (2005) summarized the results of a questionnaire distributed in 2003 to domestic institutional investors in Japan. This questionnaire serves as the basis for the questionnaire we utilize in our research. In the above-mentioned paper, Suto and Toshino found that fund managers tend to sell with a shorter horizon than is optimally desirable. Furthermore, their research demonstrates that fund managers show herding behavior. Regarding these results, the authors point out that one explanation for such behavioral characteristics is the pressure placed on fund managers by their clients. Based on information from the same questionnaire, Toshino and Suto (2004) found that Japanese institutional investors occasionally predict optimistically (or bullishly) on market returns, and that this behavioral tendency is more apparent when their predictions are based on the domestic market.

Suto, Menkhoff and Beckmann (2005) analyzed the results of a questionnaire conducted in both the US and Germany that are identical to the survey we used. Their analyses indicated that fund managers in the US tend to be more myopic, show stronger herding behavior, and demonstrate higher risk aversion than their counterparts in Germany.

Hiruma and Ikeda (2006) have investigated the factors that affect time-discounting rates as well as the impact of time-discounting rates on individual behavior. They find that a time discounting rate increases when the amount of money that must be paid out is smaller (money amount effect). Furthermore, this rate is significantly higher if the inter-temporal choice is made at a nearer point in time as opposed to a later point in time (dual discount phenomenon).

Misumi, Shumway and Takahashi (2006) have empirically explored disposition effect using Japanese on-line investor data provided by a Japanese securities company. Their results suggest that disposition effect does exist, and that investor irrationality may be its cause.

The questionnaire we utilized for this paper contains questions pertaining to the subjective risk attitudes of individual fund managers as well as their corresponding objective risk attitudes generated by expected utility theory. A question we pose that directly asks fund managers whether they consider themselves to be risk lovers, risk neutral, or risk averters directly exposes each manager's subjective risk attitude. As for the problem based on expected utility theory, we provide questions that pose hypothetical investment opportunities in which there is variance in expected return value. This allows us to measure the theoretical risk attitude of each respondent. We refer to this type of attitude as 'objective risk attitude'.

Consistency of risk attitude can be determined in the following manner. First, we measure the subjective and objective risk attitudes of each respondent based on the method outlined in the previous paragraph. If these two types of risk attitude are the same, for example, when a subjective risk averter answers the questionnaire in a manner consistent with an objective risk averter, then he or she will be called a 'risk consistent' fund manager.

There is also the possibility that a fund manager is 'risk inconsistent'. All the respondents to our questionnaire are professional fund managers. Therefore, we can predict that all the respondents have specialized knowledge concerning risk within the investment field. With this in mind, respondents should theoretically be 'risk consistent' fund managers. However, for example, if a respondent states that they are a subjective risk averter, yet demonstrates through their responses that they are an objective risk lover, they will be considered a 'risk inconsistent' fund manager. We found two types of risk inconsistency in our analysis. The fund manager mentioned above, whose subjective and objective risk attitudes don't match each other represents the first type of 'risk inconsistent' respondent. As for the second type, some fund managers inconsistently answer multiple problems on the questionnaire based on expected utility theory. For example, a respondent will choose an answer that demonstrates risk aversion in first problem, but choose a risk neutral answer in the second problem. Therefore, there are two types of risk inconsistency that appeared in our research.

Later, we will explore the two different types of respondents, 'risk consistent' and 'risk inconsistent' fund managers. As mentioned in the previous paragraph, there are two varieties of 'risk inconsistent' managers. In our analysis, we take up only the second type of risk inconsistency, that is, we will focus our attention only on objective risk attitudes. The rationale for this is that we want to know how 'risk consistent' and 'risk inconsistent' managers choose from alternatives concerning risk. With this objective in mind, we think the second type of 'risk inconsistent' manager described above can be included within the first type of risk inconsistency.

Risk inconsistency in fund managers may cause some objective and subjective differences in their preferences regarding the most important factors affecting investment. Therefore, it might be expected for such fund managers to invest in irrational ways. At the very least, it would not be going too far to assume that 'risk inconsistent' fund managers might invest more irrationally than 'risk consistent' managers.

In this paper, we look at the characteristics of herding and disposition effect, which we consider to be irrational investment behavior. When facing an unanticipated situation, 'risk inconsistent' fund managers may not be self-conscious, thus they may pay too much attention to the reactions of their colleagues or other fund managers. If this is the case, other fund managers may affect 'risk inconsistent' fund manager's investment actions in these situations. This may be the root of herding behavior. Disposition effect refers to asymmetric assessment for upward and downward price change. This is also an irrational investment act. Therefore, in this paper we will investigate the investment characteristics of Japanese professional fund managers by paying close attention to the two above-mentioned behavioral biases that have recently been the subject of a considerable amount of behavioral finance literature. The data we use is from a questionnaire-type survey conducted in 2005. The respondents were all fund managers working at Japanese institutional investment companies.

The remainder of this paper is structured as follows: In second section, we will explain our questionnaire in more detail. The third section explains our empirical model while the fourth section discusses the results.

2. Brief Summary of Questionnaire-Type Survey

This questionnaire-type survey was conducted in 2005. All respondents were fund managers of investment trusts and pension funds in Japanese trust and investment banks. We sent questionnaires to each respondent by mail and requested for them to send the questionnaires back to us. We collected 283 questionnaires out of 823 .

The questions are divided into four sections. In section 1, we ask about the respondent's background. In section 2, we ask about the relationship between operation performance and incentives. The third section features general questions on fund managing operations. In the final section, we ask respondents about their investment behavior and information gathering process[1].

3. Empirical Method and Results

In our paper, we divide all respondents into two groups; 'Risk-inconsistent' fund managers and 'risk consistent' fund managers. We investigate the differences between these two groups in terms of herding and disposition effect. In section 3.1, we define the risk consistent fund manager in detail. This paper's hypothesis is discussed in section 3.2. We conduct statistical evaluations on the differences between these two groups in section 3.3. In section 3.4, we use an ordered probit model to test our hypothesis, using each fund manager's background as a control.

3.1 Definition of a 'risk consistent' fund manager

We utilize the four questions below in order to define a 'risk consistent' fund manager.

4. Evaluation of investment behavior and information gathering processes

(11) Suppose you play a game such as 'coin toss' in which the probability of winning is 50%. If you have to pay 10 thousand yen if you lose the game, could you tell us what financial reward you would hope to get when playing this game?

_____ × 10 thousand yen or more

---

[1] A summary of our survey is reported in Toshino (2006).

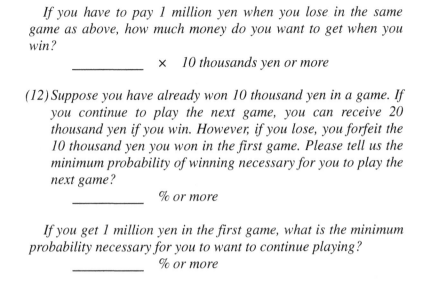

If you have to pay 1 million yen when you lose in the same game as above, how much money do you want to get when you win?

_____ × *10 thousands yen or more*

(12) Suppose you have already won 10 thousand yen in a game. If you continue to play the next game, you can receive 20 thousand yen if you win. However, if you lose, you forfeit the 10 thousand yen you won in the first game. Please tell us the minimum probability of winning necessary for you to play the next game?

_____ *% or more*

If you get 1 million yen in the first game, what is the minimum probability necessary for you to want to continue playing?

_____ *% or more*

A 'risk neutral' fund manager should set answers of 1 and 100 in question 4-(11), and 50 for question 4-(12), regardless of the amount of reward. Likewise, risk averse (or lover) fund managers should set more (or less) than 1 in the first part of question 4-(11), and more (or less) than 100 in the second part of the question. Furthermore, risk averse and risk lover managers should set more (or less) than 50 in both parts of question 4-(12), regardless of the amount of reward. If a fund manager is risk consistent, they will show the same risk attitude (answering with consistent numbers) in all questions. We can thus define such fund managers as 'risk consistent'. 'Risk inconsistent' fund managers are defined as respondents whose answers are inconsistent.

3.2 Hypothesis

As we have already discussed, research within the field of behavioral finance has developed dramatically in recent years. In this paper, we investigate the investment behavior of 'risk consistent' and 'risk inconsistent' fund managers, paying special attention to two important behavioral characteristics, herding and disposition effect.

3.2.1 Disposition effect

Misumi, Shumway and Takahashi (2006) have shown that disposition effect exists in Japanese investors. However, their research utilizes data only from on-line trades made primarily by private investors. In contrast to this, the data analyzed in our research comes entirely from professional fund managers.

We have constructed a hypothesis on disposition effect. Because their subjective and objective risk attitudes are not consistent, 'risk inconsistent' fund managers might not be able to rationally assess upward and downward price movement of investments.

> *H1:*   *'Risk consistent' fund managers show weaker disposition effect phenomenon than 'risk inconsistent' fund manager.*

3.2.2 Herding behavior

Toshino and Suto (2004) as well as Suto and Toshino (2005) have shown that herding behavior is evident in fund managers at Japanese investment institutions. The reason for this is partially due to pressure from their customers as well as their institution of employment.

In our paper, we postulate that herding behavior only exists in 'risk inconsistent' fund managers. If a fund manager understands what they need to do when facing a contingent situation in terms of risk management, he or she can take action independently. Suppose a fund manager thinks that they are a risk averter, yet, at the same time answers questions 4-(11) and 4-(12) in the manner of a risk lover. Such a 'risk inconsistent' fund manager does not fully understand his or her own risk attitude. Subjectively, he or she thinks that they are a risk averter, yet cannot choose an answer that matches this behavior in a theoretical setting. This implies that he or she might take on the behavior of a risk lover when facing a contingent situation. Furthermore, if this kind of fund manager displays anxiety about his or her risk attitude in the manner of the example above, he or she will heavily rely on their colleagues or outside information when taking investment action. This could possibly cause herding behavior in the market.

H2: '*Risk inconsistent' fund managers show a stronger phenomenon of herding behavior than 'risk consistent' fund managers.*

3.3 Descriptive statistics

3.3.1 Risk attitudes of individual fund managers

Before analyzing the differences between the investment behavior of 'risk consistent' fund managers and 'risk inconsistent' fund managers, we will investigate the general characteristics of risk attitude in our respondents. In Table.1, we show frequency distribution of responses to question 4-(11). The highest class of responses in the case of 10 thousand yen is 1 to 2 thousand yen. For the question involving 1 million yen, most responses were between 1-2 million yen. In both cases, there seems to be a high percentage of risk averters among our respondents. However, the relative frequency of the case of over 1 to 2 million yen is bigger than that of over 1 to 2 thousand yen. This means that the fund managers want to gain larger rewards when the amount they need to give up upon a loss increases. Therefore, we can say that the more a fund manager invests, the more they demonstrate risk-averting behavior.

Based on our questionnaire, we were able to define about 10% of our respondents as risk neutral. Less than 1% of the fund managers polled demonstrated risk lover behavior.

Table 1 : Frequency distribution for 4-(11)

bet(JPY)		10,000		1 million	
		frequency	relative frequency	frequency	relative frequency
Minimum probability of win	~50%	11	4.3%	10	4.0%
	50%	105	41.5%	61	24.3%
	50~60%	64	25.3%	39	15.5%
	60~70%	41	16.2%	41	16.3%
	70~80%	20	7.9%	47	18.7%
	80%~	12	4.7%	53	21.1%
total		253	100%	251	100%

Table 2 shows frequency distribution for 4-(12). As in question 4-(11), the results for 4-(12) demonstrate that the share of the risk-averting fund managers increases as the possible capital losses they would incur simultaneously increases. The share of risk neutral fund managers is larger than that of question 4-(11). This is especially true in the case of the 10 thousand yen game, in which 40% of respondents displayed risk neutral behavior. This percentage of fund managers showing risk neutral behavior is more than three times higher than that of question 4-(11).

Table 2 : Frequency of distribution for 4-(12)

Loss when lose(JPY)		10,000			1 million	
		frequency	relative frequency		frequency	relative frequency
Premium when win(JPY)	~10,000	1	0.4%	~1 mil	2	0.8%
	10,000	34	13.4%	1 mil	27	10.9%
	10,000~20,000	132	52.0%	1~2 mil	98	39.5%
	20,000~50,000	51	20.1%	2~5 mil	51	20.6%
	50,000~100,000	26	10.2%	5~10 mil	35	14.1%
	100000~	10	3.9%	10 mil	35	14.1%
total		254	100%		248	100%

3.3.2 Difference in disposition effect

In this section, we explore the difference in disposition effect between 'risk consistent' and 'risk inconsistent' fund managers. Responses to questions 4-(1)-① and 4-(1)-⑤ are analyzed.

4. Assessment of investment behavior and information gathering processes

(1) Please describe your investment behavior. Choose 1 for behavior you agree strongly with, and 6 for behavior you don't agree with. In this manner, please rate each behavior from 1 to 6.

① *Suppose you face an accidental liquidity shortage and need to sell some assets. You would prefer to sell assets in the black as opposed to assets in the red.*

⑤ *It is preferable for you to wait for price recovery when your asset is in the red as opposed to fixing the loss yourself.*

Table 3 shows a summary of the responses to questions related to disposition effect. The number of fund managers who set 3 and 6 is relatively high. That is, the shape of distribution is diphasic. Furthermore, the responses of 'risk consistent' fund managers seem to be higher. The median response of 'risk consistent' fund managers is 4, while that of 'risk inconsistent' fund managers is 3. Using Wilcoxon test, the distribution between 'risk consistent' and 'risk inconsistent' fund managers can be seen to be significantly different for question 4-1-①, which has a 5% level, and question 4-1-⑤, which has only a 1% level.

Analyzing the above results, it is evident that the tendency of disposition effect in 'risk consistent' fund managers is weaker than that of 'risk inconsistent' fund managers.

Table 3 : Summary of responses to disposition effect related questions

Question		1	2	3	4	5	6	total	median	p-value
4-1-①	risk consistent	3	19	34	27	17	43	143	4	
	risk inconsistent	5	22	30	11	14	23	105	3	
	total	8	41	64	38	31	66	248		0.026
4-1-⑤	risk consistent	0	18	33	33	27	30	141	4	
	risk inconsistent	5	23	32	11	17	18	106	3	
	total	5	41	65	44	44	48	247		0.006

p-value is the p-value of the wilcoxon ranksum test.

3.3.3 *Difference in herding behavior*

Below, we will analyze questions 4-(3)-④~⑧ and 4-(4) to investigate the difference in herding behavior between 'risk consistent' and 'risk inconsistent' fund managers.

4. Assessment of investment behavior and information gathering Processes

(3) *When you need to reach an investment decision, how important to you are the following information gathering processes? Choose 1 for information very important to you, and 6 for information that is not important to you. In this manner, rate each behavior from 1 to 6.*

④ *Discussion and exchange of opinions with colleague :*

⑤ *Opinion of analyst and strategist inside your institution :*

⑥ *Investment decision of other market participant :*
⑦ *Opinions of leader in the same industry (eg.:Warren Edward Buffett) :*
⑧ *Opinions of leader in the business world (eg.:Ben S.Bernanke) :*

(4) When your opinion differs from your colleagues or opinion leaders, which do you attach a higher value to? If you attach a higher value to your own decision, please choose 1. If you attach a higher value to others, choose 6. You can thus rate your behavior from 1 to 6.

Table 4 : Summary of questions regarding herding behavior

Question		1	2	3	4	5	6	total	median	p-value
4-(3)-④	risk consistent	26	47	39	21	8	2	143	2	
	risk inconsistent	23	35	31	10	5	3	107	2	
	total	49	82	70	31	13	5	250		0.45
4-(3)-⑤	risk consistent	36	49	34	14	9	1	143	2	
	risk inconsistent	18	35	31	11	9	3	107	3	
	total	54	84	65	25	18	4	250		0.07
4-(3)-⑥	risk consistent	3	21	52	40	19	8	143	3	
	risk inconsistent	3	19	40	15	21	9	107	3	
	total	6	40	92	55	40	17	250		0.91
4-(3)-⑦	risk consistent	1	8	41	39	33	21	143	4	
	risk inconsistent	0	5	25	33	26	18	107	4	
	total	1	13	66	72	59	39	250		0.33
4-(3)-⑧	risk consistent	17	35	45	20	19	7	143	3	
	risk inconsistent	4	24	28	26	16	9	107	3	
	total	21	59	73	46	35	16	250		0.01
4-(4)	risk consistent	43	67	27	6	0	0	143	2	
	risk inconsistent	40	32	29	3	0	1	105	2	
	total	83	99	56	9	0	1	248		0.92

p-value is the p-value of the wilcoxon ranksum test.

Table 4 shows the summary of response results to the above questions. In almost all of the questions, we cannot find any difference in the distribution of answers between 'risk consistent' and 'risk inconsistent' fund managers. Only in question 4-(3)-⑧ is a significant difference evident (5%). However, this question is regarding the importance of opinions held by leaders in the business world, which even 'risk consistent' fund managers attach a high value to. This implies that the behavior of 'risk consistent' fund managers may also follow herding. This result goes against our hypothesis.

3.4 *Ordered probit analysis*

In the analysis of the previous section, the tendency of disposition effect in 'risk inconsistent' fund managers appeared to be stronger than that of 'risk consistent' fund managers. However, we need to be careful in reaching a conclusion. We must exclude elements such as individual background, which may affect the above results. In this section, we will estimate an ordered probit model to control these elements as well as to better explore the behavioral characteristics of professional fund managers in Japan.

3.4.1 *Model*

In questions 4-(1)-① and 4-(1)-⑤, which investigate disposition effect, respondents must choose an integer from 1 to 6. If these answers are in ratio scale or interval scale, we can use OLS. However, since we cannot be certain of their scale, and because all of the responses are in integer form, we employ an ordered probit model.

Suppose an unobservable latent variable y_i^* can be determined by the linear expression consisting of AGE_i, $EXPR_i$, $NEXPR_i$, $RSRCH_i$, $WORK_i$, $SWTCH_i$, DC_i.

$$y_i^* = \beta_1 AGE_i + \beta_2 EXPR_i + \beta_3 NEXPR_i + \beta_4 RSRCH_i \\ + \beta_5 WORK_i + \beta_6 SWTCH_i + \beta_7 DC_i + \varepsilon_i \tag{1}$$

Here, the variables

AGE_i, $EXPR_i$, $NEXPR_i$, $RSRCH_i$, $WORK_i$, $SWTCH_i$, are the age of respondent i ,(1-(3)), the length of work experience in the fund investment industry (1-(4)), the length of work experience in the company now he or she belongs to (1-(4-1)), average working hours per week (1-(5)), time for data processing and research (1-(6)), the number of career switches so far (1-(4-2)), and DC_i is a dummy variable. DC_i takes 1 if the i th respondent is a 'risk consistent' fund manager, otherwise 0. ε_i is an error term with normal distribution.

The answer of i th respondent is dependent on y_i^* and this relationship can be expressed as below.

$$y_i = \begin{cases} 1 & \text{if } y_i^* \le \gamma_1 \\ 2 & \text{if } \gamma_1 < y_i^* \le \gamma_2 \\ \vdots & \vdots \\ 6 & \text{if } \gamma_6 \le y_i^* \end{cases} \qquad (2)$$

Here, $\gamma_1,...,\gamma_6$ and $\beta_0,...,\beta_7$ are parameters to be estimated.

The larger y_i^* becomes, the larger y_i also becomes. Therefore, y_i^* can represent disposition effect even though y_i is a latent variable of i th respondent. The smaller value of y_i^* implies stronger disposition effect. In addition, y_i^* is modeled as depending on the individual background and risk consistency so that the estimated value of $\beta_1,...,\beta_7$ can be used to test whether these factors statistically affect the level of disposition effect or not.

For estimating our model, we use EViews (Quantitative Micro Software (2004)).

3.4.2 *Estimation results*

In Table 5, we show estimation results for the ordered probit model related to disposition effect. As for individual background, almost all variables are not significant at the 5% level. Only the result for question 4-(1)-⑤, the parameter of research time, is significantly estimated at the 5% level and positive. This result shows that fund managers whose research time is longer have a weaker tendency to wait for price recovery. However, all other individual background factors do not appear to have any influence on disposition effect.

As for the risk consistency dummy result, the parameters DC_i in both questions are estimated significantly at the 1% level and positive.

From these results, we can confirm that 'risk consistent' fund managers show smaller disposition effect than their 'risk inconsistent' counterparts. Thus, here we can reaffirm the results attained in section 3.2.

Table 5 : Estimation results of ordered probit model on disposition effect

	Q. 4-(1)-①		Q. 4-(1)-⑤	
	coefficient	Standerd error	coefficient	Standerd error
AGE	-0.009	(0.0193)	-0.003	(0.0215)
EXPR	0.013	(0.0196)	-0.006	(0.0211)
NEXPR	0.020	(0.0159)	0.022	(0.0153)
RSRCH	0.010	(0.0067)	0.016	(0.0069)*
WORK	-0.007	(0.0081)	-0.012	(0.0088)
SWTCH	0.111	(0.0956)	0.180	(0.0928)**
DC	0.432	(0.1506)***	0.412	(0.1502)***

***,**,* denote statistical significance at th 1%, 5% and 10% level respectively.

Table 6 : Estimation results of ordered probit model on herding behavior

	Q. 4-(3)-④		Q. 4-(3)-⑤		Q. 4-(3)-⑥	
	coefficient	standerd error	coefficient	standerd error	coefficient	standerd error
AGE	0.018	(0.0243)	0.019	(0.0248)	0.012	(0.0208)
EXPR	0.001	(0.0263)	-0.003	(0.0259)	0.013	(0.0227)
NEXPR	-0.014	(0.0196)	-0.020	(0.0181)	0.024	(0.0178)
RSRCH	-0.014	(0.0069)**	0.010	(0.0080)	0.024	(0.0079)***
WORK	-0.020	(0.0110)*	0.004	(0.0087)	-0.018	(0.0120)
SWTCH	0.216	(0.0953)**	0.143	(0.1187)	0.144	(0.0960)
DC	0.253	(0.1765)	-0.228	(0.1797)	0.152	(0.1792)

	Q. 4-(3)-⑦		Q. 4-(3)-⑧		Q. 4-(4)	
	coefficient	standerd error	coefficient	standerd error	coefficient	standerd error
AGE	0.006	(0.0236)	0.009	(0.0238)	-0.017	(0.0251)
EXPR	-0.010	(0.0244)	-0.001	(0.0257)	0.004	(0.0267)
NEXPR	0.006	(0.0197)	0.028	(0.0181)	-0.014	(0.0176)
RSRCH	0.015	(0.0075)**	0.005	(0.0074)	-0.020	(0.0076)***
WORK	0.000	(0.0094)	0.009	(0.0083)	0.000	(0.0107)
SWTCH	0.135	(0.1114)	-0.057	(0.1339)	-0.011	(0.1329)
DC	0.039	(0.1779)	-0.237	(0.1753)	-0.375	(0.1934)*

***,**,* denote statistical significance at th 1%, 5% and 10% level respectively.

In Table 6, we show estimation results for the ordered probit model related to herding behavior.

The dummy variables that are significantly estimated at a 10% level only exist in question 4-(4). Because the values of these are all minus, it can be seen that 'risk consistent' fund managers tend to place more trust in their own investment decisions and show less herding behavior than 'risk inconsistent' fund managers.

The results in Chap.3.3.3, in which personal background is not controlled, shows that questions 4-(3)-⑤ and 4-(3)-⑧ are significant at the 10% level. However, the dummy variables in the ordered probit model are not significant. From these statistics, the results in Chap.3.3.3 might be considered pseudo results, as there was no control for the backgrounds of each fund manager.

Continuing our analysis of personal backgrounds, results regarding research hours are significant in questions 4-(3)-④、 4-(3)-⑥、 4-(3)-⑦、 4-④ at the 5% level. The signs of these results are plus in questions 4-(3)-⑥ and 4-(3)-⑦, and minus in 4-(3)-④ and 4-④. These results show that fund managers whose research hours are long do not pay much attention to the behavior of other market participants. Furthermore, these fund managers tend to care about the opinions of their colleagues and place much trust in their own decisions. Therefore, such fund managers do not seem to demonstrate herding behavior, as they do not follow how other market participants invest.

4. Summary

In this research paper, we investigated risk consistency and other investment behaviors of fund managers working at Japanese investment institutions using a questionnaire based survey that was conducted in October of 2005. In particular, we focused on the herding behavior and disposition effect of fund managers. This research utilized the results of numerous research papers from the field of behavioral finance.

We began by investigating the attitudes towards risk held by fund managers. We then divided them into two groups: 'risk consistent' fund managers and 'risk inconsistent' fund managers. In exploring the difference in investment behavior between these two groups, we found that 'risk inconsistent' fund managers have a tendency to show disposition behavior. As for herding behavior, we could not find any strong evidence that might indicate a difference between the two groups.

To further our research, we took a closer look at the disposition effect that we found in our preliminary analysis. Because we could not ignore the influence of each fund manger's individual background, we estimated an ordered probit model to control individual characteristics. After controlling individual information, we were able to confirm that 'risk inconsistent' fund managers show disposition effect.

References

[1]   Hiruma, Fumihiko and Shunsuke Ikeda (2006), research on time discount rate based on economic experiments and questionnaire-type survey (written in Japanese), PRI Discussion Paper Series , No.06A-26.

[2]   Misumi, Takashi, Tyler Shumway, and Hidetomo Takahashi(2006), Are Japanese Individual Investors Subject to the Behavioral Disposition Effect?, The 5th behavioral economics workshop, Aoyama Gakuin University..

[3]   Quantitative Micro Software(2004), *EViews5 User's Guide.*

[4]   Suto, Megumi, Lukas Menkhoff, and Daniela Beckmann(2005), Behavioral Biases of Institutional Investors under Pressure from Customers: Japan and Germany vs the US, *Waseda University Institute of Finance Working Paper Series* WIF-05-006.

[5]   Suto, Megumi, and Masashi Toshino(2005), Behavioral Biases of Japanese Institutional Investors: fund management and corporate governance, *Corporate Governance: An International Review* 13, 466-477.

[6]   Toshino, Masashi, and Megumi Suto(2004), Cognitive Biases of Japanese Institutional Investors: Consistency with Behavioral Finance, *Waseda University Institute of Finance Working Paper Series* WIF-04-005.

[7]   Toshino, Masahi(2006), fund manager consciousness survey -preliminary results- (written in Japanese), mimeo